THE
GOLFER'S BIBLE

THE GOLFER'S BIBLE

REVISED EDITION

Frank Kenyon Allen, Dale Mead,
Tom Lo Presti, and Barbara Romack

Revised by John Andrisani

Doubleday

New York London Toronto Sydney Auckland

All photographs by Leonard Kamsler.

Excerpts from *The Rules of Golf* reprinted with permission of the United States Golf Association

Published by Doubleday, a division of Bantam Doubleday Dell Publishing Group, Inc., 666 Fifth Avenue, New York, New York 10103

Doubleday and the portrayal of an anchor with a dolphin are trademarks of Doubleday, a division of Bantam Doubleday Dell Publishing Group, Inc.

Designed by Rhea Braunstein

Library of Congress Cataloging-in-Publication Data
Allen, Frank Kenyon.
  The golfer's bible / Frank Kenyon Allen, Tom Lo Presti, and
Barbara Romack ; revised by John Andrisani. — Rev. ed.
     p. cm.
  1. Golf. I. Lo Presti, Tom.   II. Romack, Barbara.
III. Andrisani, John.   IV. Title.
GV965.A48 1989
796.352′3—dc19   88-14827
                                                            CIP

ISBN 0-385-24102-X

ACKNOWLEDGMENTS

Thanks are due to Leonard Kamsler, renowned New York-based photographer, for taking the wonderful shots that complement the text.

Thanks also to Robert Geambazi, head golf professional at Ridgewood Country Club, in Danbury, Connecticut, for modeling, and for his wholehearted cooperation in furnishing the equipment and other material, together with price ranges, featured in Chapter 6.

Contents

Introduction

Much has been written on perfecting one's game of golf. To provide all the instructional advice necessary for proper performance, including proper grip, stance and alignment, the basic swing, wood shots, iron play, trouble shots, and the many other phases of this wonderful game, would require a volume too massive to be practical. The average golfer simply could not absorb so much instruction at one time.

Our belief is that the best way to approach learning golf is *one step at a time,* with the help of a good PGA teaching professional. The "physical" instruction should start by focusing on *one step.* Next, the player should concentrate on this teaching during practice until he feels he has mastered this one step. Then he should return to his professional to review his performance, and to further refine his golf shot execution.

It is not unusual, however, for the player to forget or misconstrue parts of the instructions, with the result that the faulty execution of the past creeps back in, and the value of the instruction is virtually lost. This is one of the reasons why most teaching professionals prefer not to cover more than one subject during a single lesson. Likewise, we agree and suggest that the reader of this book concentrate on one subject at a time and not try to master the whole game overnight. Trying to do so will only lead to frustration.

This book is designed to provide beginning and intermediate golfers with a concise, step-by-step handbook that will *supplement* the instruction they receive from golf professionals. To get the full value from the steps outlined:

1. Memorize each point in order to form a clear mental picture of a good swing.

2. Practice each step separately, until the proper technique becomes ingrained in your muscle-memory.

3. See a professional teacher at least once a month to keep your swing tuned.

If you follow this procedure, and you concentrate, it's a good bet that you will have complete confidence in your ability to execute golf shots well during actual play. With such confidence, relaxation, so essential to proper execution of all golf shots, is assured.

But remember, if you wish to excel at *anything,* you must *work* at it—systematically.

A good many people have been heard to say, "I don't want to take the game so seriously—I don't want to take the time to study and memorize the technique." Our answer to that is: okay, then be satisfied to join the ranks of about 90 percent of the 22 million golfers in this country who very seldom, if ever, score in the 80s, and many of whom never break 100 around 18 holes.

Our guess is that *you* are different, that you have

the motivation to do what is necessary to become a top-flight player of golf. Try it! And find out how easy it is to quickly become one of the top 10 percent—a low handicap golfer whose skill matches his enthusiasm.

NOTE: The execution techniques described in these pages, as well as the illustrations, are designed for *right-handed* players. Left-handed players should simply reverse positions.

THE
GOLFER'S BIBLE

1

The Basic Swing

For each step above, a simple chronology of the techniques is outlined, then illustrated, and then each point is explained in subsequent pages. The explanations are for your reference.

Study and *memorize* the simple techniques outlined for each step. Then make up your mind that each time you step up to your ball, you will relax and execute your swing precisely according to plan. If you have done your work well, you will be surprised how easily things begin to fall into place.

Your golf instructor will probably start you swinging with a No. 6 or No. 7 iron instead of a wood club, because the irons are easier to swing. While we have no quarrel with this practice, we have started description of the techniques of the basic swing with the No. 1 wood or driver.

While the swing with the longer wood clubs is a little more difficult, you won't get to use the shorter irons too often unless you learn to drive the ball off the tee.

THE STANDARD GRIP

What to Do

1. Take your grip in the *left* hand first, with the left thumb resting firmly on the upper right side of the club's handle, and the other fingers (particularly the last three) gripping firmly, *but not tensely,* and seeing that only two or three knuckles show when you're looking down on this hand.

2. Place your right hand against the clubshaft with the palm square to the target, and with the thumb on the *upper left* of the shaft.

3. Cradle the club's handle *across* the forefinger of the right hand, and rest the end of the thumb on this finger. Applying pressure of the thumb and forefinger on the club's handle contributes greatly to the feel of a good grip. Also, it helps to assure correct alignment of the clubhead (square to the target) throughout the entire swing. *Under no circumstances* should you allow the right forefinger to extend loosely against the right side of the shaft, as so many high handicappers do.

4. Now complete the right-hand grip with the two middle fingers. Finally, rest the little finger of the right hand atop the forefinger of the left hand. After completing the grip, see that the "Vs" formed between thumbs and forefingers of *both* hands are pointing toward the *right* shoulder.

TAILORING THE TIP

Golfers whose hands are small should consider either an interlocking or baseball grip, as each provides more security than the overlapping (Vardon) hold. Basically, the interlocking hold is formed by entwining the little finger of the right hand between the first and second fingers of the left hand. The baseball grip places all fingers of both hands on the club's handle.

How to Do It

For consistent direction control, point the V (formed by the thumb and forefinger of your left, or "lead" hand), at your right shoulder.

For a more secure hold on the club, put more pressure on the last three fingers of your left hand.

To protect against placing your right hand in too powerful a position, set its palm parallel to your left palm.

To promote maximum feel for the clubhead—and shot—let the right thumb and forefinger pinch each other.

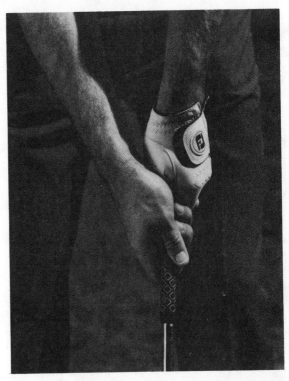

The "ready" position: V's pointing to the right shoulder; right palm parallel to the left palm; back of the left hand square to the target.

Why You Do It

ITEM 1. Unless a golfer learns to properly grip his clubs, there is little or no assurance that he will be able to execute good golf shots consistently. Developing a proper grip is the first step in setting up a correct swing pattern.

When the left-hand grip on the club's handle allows two or three finger knuckles to be seen by the player, a secure grip is created, providing good left-hand control of the club. The "V" formed between the left thumb and forefinger should point toward the *right* shoulder.

Placing this hand too far to the left on the handle creates a weak grip, generally resulting in loss of distance, and contributing to a sliced shot.

A firm, but not tense grip (principally with the last three fingers of the left hand) promotes good club control, and prevents the fatal error of loosening the grip at the top of the backswing. Recessing the grip of the left hand on the handle approximately 1 inch from the end will help to prevent the grip from loosening at the top of the backswing, and further promote good club control and direction of the ball's flight.

To match the top Tour pros, copy the most popular grip (Vardon), by letting your right pinkie rest atop your left forefinger or between the first and second fingers of your left hand.

In addition, when playing iron shots from the fairway, where a divot must be taken, a firm grip with the left hand reduces the chance that the clubface will open up with the shock of impact. Should this happen, a severe sliced shot would most likely result.

ITEM 2. It's critical to keep the palm of the right hand facing the target during the initial gripping of the club with the right hand when addressing the ball, and at the point of impact with the ball in the downswing.

Actually, when the *right*-hand grip is completed, this hand is placed slightly under the club's handle, with the right arm relaxed. No finger knuckles of this hand should be seen by the player. Also, *under no circumstances* should the thumb be placed straight down on *top* of the handle.

ITEM 3. A great deal of the control in the grip of the right hand is provided by the pressure of the thumb and first two fingers. The right thumb should be placed firmly *across* the shaft's handle to the *upper left side,* and with pressure of the first thumb joint applied to the handle. The forefinger should be *slightly* extended (like pulling the trigger of a pistol), and crooked around the handle with pressure applied by the second joint of this finger. The handle is therefore cradled across this finger, which should now be allowed to touch the end of the thumb.

ITEM 4. To complete the right-hand grip, the *left* thumb is snugly fitted into the heel of the palm of the right hand; the pressure of the fleshy base of the right thumb against the left thumb should be maintained throughout the entire swing. The more closely together the two hands are placed, the better the control of the club throughout.

Finally, assuming the most popular grip is used, the (Vardon) overlap, place the *little* finger of the right hand over the *forefinger* of the left hand. The "V" between the thumb and forefinger of both hands should now point toward the right shoulder.

Be a "Square" at Address

If your hands are in the correct position on the club, it's easier to hit the ball straight. Correct is when the palms of both hands are "square" to the target: To check, take your grip and, without changing position, open your fingers: the palm of the right hand and the back of the left should be facing the target. This "neutral" grip is best because it positions the hands to return naturally to a square position at impact. If you set up with a square clubface and a neutral grip, you're more likely to hit the ball straight.

We suggest that you see your school instructor or PGA teaching professional for advice on the proper grip for you, before you become too accustomed to one which may not be suitable for your particular needs. It is sometimes difficult to change. Then, once you determine your "stronghold," practice both with and without swinging your clubs, until you automatically grip them the same way every time you use them.

THE STANCE

The square stance is recommended for most golfers.

NOTE: *Before* positioning the feet, place the clubhead behind the ball, *square* to the intended flight line, with the sole of the clubhead *flat* on the ground. *Then* position the feet.

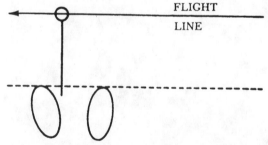

This finds the toes of both feet *even* with an imaginary line parallel to the flight line.

The open stance is used when playing an intentional fade or sliced shot.

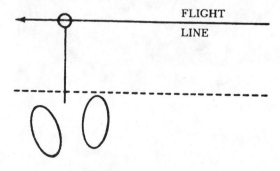

It is also used when the shorter irons are played, since there is less body turn, and a more upright swing arc.

The closed stance is used when playing an intentional hook or draw shot, from *right* to *left*.

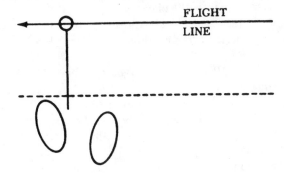

It is also a help to some older players, who find it difficult to get sufficient body turn in the backswing.

THE TEE SHOT

The Same Way—Every Time

The authors refer to this part of the instruction for the swing as the "basic" swing, because it covers the fundamental procedures essential to proper performance in the tee shot on a *consistent* basis.

Quite likely, many of us have noticed that certain amateur players seem to be able to consistently "keep their ball in play." Their golf shots off the tee, or on the fairway, seem to always be "down the middle," and straight for the target or objective point.

Why is this?

We believe it is because such players have firmly fixed in their minds the *techniques* which *must be considered in every shot,* and the proper *sequence* in which these things should be employed.

The next and most important factor in their success is that each time they address their ball, they make sure that everything pertinent to that particular shot has been carefully considered, and as a result, they do the *same things* the *same way every time.*

We fully recognize the variations in the manner in which certain golf shots must be executed, in cases where hazards must be overcome, or when playing certain of the shorter irons.

This does not apply to the tee shot, however, where the execution should always be the same, essentially, with regards to heeding particular evergreen fundamentals.

In the following pages, a step-by-step chronology of the techniques for the tee shot is outlined. Make up your mind that you are going to learn them. Not the words necessarily, but the techniques themselves—and the proper sequence in the execution. Then, every time that you step up to the teeing area to make your drive, check in your mind quickly *what* you are supposed to do, and *do it.* Once this review has been accomplished, pull the trigger.

STEP 1. STANCE AND ADDRESS

What to Do

1. Tee the ball (with one half of the ball above the clubhead when it is grounded).

2. Step back and line up the target from behind the ball.

3. Grip the club, as indicated on preceding pages. Grip with the left hand first.

4. Place the clubhead behind the ball with the sole *flat* on ground, and the clubface square to the target. The right-hand grip is completed after taking the proper stance.

5. Take the stance as follows:
   A. The ball is positioned opposite the *instep* of the *left foot.*
   B. The left shoulder is pointing toward the target.
   C. The weight is equally on the heels and soles of the feet. The right foot is pointed slightly to the right for a fuller turn on the backswing.
   D. The left toe is pointed out more than the right foot to provide good balance on the downswing.
   E. The feet are spread approximately the width of the shoulders.
   F. Flex the knees—"sit down to the ball," but *don't crouch!*
   G. Bend the upper body forward *slightly*, approximately 30 degrees.

H. The left hand, arm, and clubshaft should form a line straight from the clubhead to the left shoulder. The hands will then be just inside of the left thigh and slightly ahead of the ball.

I. Arch the wrists slightly, particularly the right. *Don't reach for the ball.*

How to Do It

To promote a clean sweep with the driver, tee up with the top half of the ball above the top of the clubface.

Why You Do It

ITEM 1. Teeing the ball as described here will enable the player to hit the ball slightly on the *upswing* at impact, near the *top* of the clubface, assuming the ball is positioned correctly, opposite the left instep.

This assures a high trajectory, which provides greater carrying distance in the ball's flight than one teed and hit low.

If the downswing is right, the ball will not be "blooped" high, and for only a short distance. However, when hitting into a headwind, the ball should be teed lower, and played more toward the center of the stance.

ITEM 2. After teeing the ball, it is a good idea to step back facing the intended flight direction, to determine where you want the ball to land, considering such things as wind direction, fairway hazards, ground slopes, etc. Then take your stance as outlined, under Item 5B on page 00.

ITEM 3. Gripping the club with the left hand only, at first, enables the player to square the clubface to the target, and to have the shaft in a straight line with the left arm and shoulder.

ITEM 4. Placing the clubhead behind the ball, square to the intended line of flight, before taking your stance, helps to assure a straight hit. It also determines how far from the ball the stance should be. *Don't reach* for the ball so that the clubhead is resting only on its heel. When the proper stance position is completed, the hips, shoulders, and clubface must be square to the target. Then complete the grip with the right hand without turning the body laterally. Should such a turn occur, the right-hand placement on the club's handle might pull the right side of the body out, changing the squareness of alignment. This could cause a hit from the outside in, resulting in either a sharply pulled shot or a slice.

ITEM 5A. Positioning the ball opposite the instep of the left foot (assuming the rest of the stance is correct) assures hitting slightly on the upswing just *after* the bottom of the downswing arc has been reached. The result is a clean, solid hit for good distance, through a high trajectory of the ball's flight.

ITEM 5B. With the left shoulder pointing toward the target, the stance should be *square* to the direction line desired. A closed stance (left foot slightly ahead of the right) induces a hooked shot, while an open stance (right foot slightly ahead of the left), contributes to more of a fade, or a slice.

Some players prefer to use either a slightly closed or slightly open stance for their tee shots, either of which may be better adapted to the individual's personal style of swing. This is often due to certain characteristics such as age, swing arc, physical deficiencies, etc. In general, however, the square stance produces the best results for most people.

ITEM 5C. When the weight is distributed equally on the heels, as well as the soles, of both feet at address, good balance in the entire swing is more easily attained. There should be a feeling of slight pres-

Address (downtarget view): Setting the feet and body square to the target and bending slightly at the knees and waist are a "must."

Address (face-on view): Making the clubshaft an extension of your left arm is paramount to promoting a smooth takeaway of the club along the target line.

sure on the insteps, but not to the extent that the body is thrown forward toward the ball in the downswing.

ITEM 5D. Pointing the right foot slightly to the right and the left foot out a little more to the left helps to unblock the hips in both the backswing and the downswing. This allows a fuller turn in the backswing, and a smooth downswing with a full follow-through without loss of balance.

ITEM 5E. For all wood shots as well as the long irons, the feet at address should be spread approximately the width of the shoulders. When the spread is less than this, the full power of the swing is lost, and the swing arc is restricted. When the spread is too wide, proper turning of the hips and shoulders is prevented in both the backswing and the down-

swing, again reducing the swing arc, and flattening the entire swing.

As the shorter clubs are used, the spread of the feet narrows, because less power is required, and the swing arc is shorter and more upright.

ITEMS 5F and G. Flexing the knees—"sitting down to the ball"—assures a firm but relaxed stance at address, putting the body in position to pivot properly without swaying. *Don't crouch!* When the knees are flexed and the shoulders slumped forward slightly, the head is pulled down, and the upper body is bent forward approximately 30 degrees. This entire body position now permits addressing the club to the ball at the proper angle and distance.

ITEM 5H. Keeping the left hand, arm, and clubshaft in a straight line from the clubhead to the left shoulder places the hands slightly *ahead* of the ball at address, as they should be for all golf shots. This allows the hands, arms, and club to start the backswing in a firm, controlled motion, preventing an early wrist break, which causes the clubhead to be picked up sharply.

Since the position of the left arm, hands, and clubhead at impact is usually the same as at address, this again places the hands ahead of the ball to lead the clubhead through and out toward the target.

ITEM 5I. When the stance is finally completed, make sure that the *right* shoulder is lower than the left at address. However, it should *not* be extended forward across the intended flight line, because this would spoil the squareness of the stance alignment. (Additional coverage of shoulder positions during the *swing* will be found in following pages.)

STEP 2. THE BACKSWING

What to Do

1. Waggle the clubhead.

2. Set the clubhead behind the ball.

3. Cock the head to the right, and make a slight forward press to the left with the hands and the right knee.

4. Start the backswing *(low* and *slow)* with a push from the left side through the hand and arm. The clubhead should be dragged away from the ball with the left arm and the clubshaft forming a straight line, and with the clubhead kept low to the ground for first 12 inches. At same time:

   A. Turn the hips to the right until the back faces the target.
   B. The left shoulder turns to the right until it drops under the chin.
   C. The left knee dips in to the right.
   D. The weight shifts to the right foot, with pressure on the *inside* of the foot.

5. KEEP THE ARMS *fully extended,* with the left arm in line with the clubshaft.

6. Keep both arms straight, and don't hinge the wrists until the hands are at least hip high.

7. Continue the backswing until the hands reach shoulder height or higher, depending on the player's ability. *Don't bend the left arm.*

8. *Keep the head still* and *both eyes on the ball.*

9. At the top of the backswing, *don't loosen the grip on the club.*

10. Keep the backswing well within your physical limits. *Don't stretch or strain.*

11. When the top of backswing is reached, start the downswing automatically, start unwinding.

How to Do It

Takeaway: Start the backswing low and slow with both arms fully extended. Don't pick up the clubhead sharply from ground; keep it low to the ground for the first 12 inches of the swing.

First Move Up: Swivel the hips to the right. Don't sway laterally.

head and chin out of the way, permitting the tilt and turn of the left shoulder. This also helps the body to take a longer, less inhibited turn than if the head were straight forward.

The forward press is a slight movement of the hands, body, and right knee to the left, setting the swing in motion as a recoil from this movement.

This also relieves tension since it is a continuation of the waggle.

The start of the backswing finds the right knee still bent slightly toward the ball, putting the weight automatically on the inside of the right foot.

ITEM 4. Starting the backswing *low* and *slow*, with the clubhead close to the ground for the first 12

At the Top: The classic position for promoting straight hits sees the clubshaft paralleling an imaginary line running from ball to target.

Why You Do It

ITEM 1. Waggling the clubhead before the start of the backswing is a combination of slight wrist, arm, and club movement to relieve tension. It also helps to start the backswing in a smooth manner.

ITEM 2. Setting the clubhead behind the ball again, just before starting the backswing, places it in the same position as at the initial address, for the correct start of the club movement.

ITEM 3. Cocking the head to the right just before the start of the backswing, like the forward press, helps to start the backswing in motion. It gets the inches, and with the left arm, hand, and clubshaft in a straight line, prevents picking up the clubhead through a collapse of the straight left arm. This results in throwing the clubhead over the right shoulder, and tends to sway the body laterally to the right.

ITEM 4A. The hips will automatically turn toward the right (making room for the club to swing freely inside the target line) if the backswing is started as described above, provided the head is kept still, and no lateral sway to the right takes place.

ITEM 4B. When the left shoulder is pulled around to the right, it lowers until it drops under the chin, while the right shoulder raises. At all times during the backswing, the upper body and the head *must* stay over the ball. (The correct position is like having a rod running through the body from top to bottom vertically, and the body pivoting around this rod.) The upper body is now coiled for a strong uncoiling action to be started by the downswing.

ITEM 4C. Dipping the left knee in to the right naturally accompanies the body pivot action, placing the left foot in position for the weight to be shifted to the inside of this foot on the downswing. *Guard against lifting the heel off the ground too far.* This could cause excessive body sway to the right in the backswing.

ITEM 4D. The weight shift to the inside of the right foot takes place naturally during the backswing pivot. It is, however, not a true weight shift, but actually a bracing of the right foot during the pivot process. Most of the weight rests on the ball of the left foot at this point. What happens is a straightening of the right knee (but not locking it), with the pivot creating a coiling action around this leg. When this coiling is released in the downswing, the right knee is thrust toward the target, providing much of the power for the hit.

ITEMS 5 and 6. Keeping both arms fully extended to the point where the hands reach to about hip level prevents picking up the clubhead sharply as described in Item 4. When this point is reached, the right elbow starts to bend in close to the right side of the body. The wrist break or cocking action

should take place naturally as the hands are raised above this level.

ITEM 7. The higher the player's hands are brought in the full backswing, the greater the swing arc, and resulting distance to be attained in the hit. However, this height must be adjusted according to the individual player's ability. Older players particularly sometimes find that their shoulder muscles are not supple enough to permit a full backswing. Generally the difference in distance to be attained between a three-quarter swing and a full backswing is only about 15 to 20 yards for most players.

ITEM 8. Keeping the head and body relatively still during the backswing prevents lateral sway, and moving away from the target. There is bound to be some movement, and the way to keep it at a minimum is to twist the body in the pivot, instead of swaying laterally. When the body and head move drastically, it is also difficult to keep the eyes on the ball. The result is a scuffed or topped shot.

ITEM 9. Loosening the grip at the top of the backswing creates "floating hands." The position of the clubhead generally is changed from what it was at address, and it is difficult, if not impossible, to regrip and correct the clubhead alignment in the downswing. When this occurs, it's virtually impossible to achieve square and solid clubface-to-ball contact at impact.

Keep pressure with the last three fingers of the left hand (particularly the little finger) on the club's handle throughout the entire swing.

ITEM 10. Don't try to stretch the backswing beyond the point of your individual ability. Again, assuming the rest of your swing is good, the difference in distance through either a full or three-quarter backswing is negligible, particularly when the player with the shorter swing develops accuracy with his drives and fairway wood and iron shots.

ITEM 11. During the entire backswing process, the upper body has been coiled for release with the power in the downswing. The start of the downswing automatically becomes the beginning of this uncoiling.

STEP 3. THE DOWNSWING

What to Do

1. Start the downswing slowly.

2. Delay the complete turn of the body toward the target to allow the hands and arms to come through.

3. Lead the club down with the left hand and arm. "Draw" the arms down with the left arm kept straight (until completely through the impact with the ball).

4. Delay uncocking of the wrists until the hands reach to about *hip level*.

5. The weight shifts to the left foot. Move the *hips* first, then the shoulders, to the left, then the arms and hands. Thrust the *right* knee to the left —*push off the inside* of the right foot.

6. The *right* elbow returns to the side *slightly in front of the body*.

7. Now uncock the wrists, snapping them into a straight line with the arms, bringing the clubhead into the ball.

8. The *right* shoulder lowers naturally (down and under) until it touches the chin.

9. *Keep the head still, and both eyes on the ball.*

SWING REMINDERS

1. Keep your swing *smooth* and *rhythmic*.
2. Don't overswing.
3. Good timing will often get more distance for you than a "slugged" shot.

How to Do It

First Move Down: Pull the arms and hands down hard toward the ball (mostly with the "left" arm). Don't be too eager to hit.

Why You Do It

ITEM 1. The speed of the backswing and the downswing should be relatively the same, as long as the entire swing is smooth. This is called timing. For some players, the swing will be faster than for others, and you must determine the cadence best suited to your style and ability. In essence, a little faster swing helps to promote a harder hit, but the player should never press or allow a jerky motion to creep in.

Swinging the shoulders around to the left too quickly could throw the clubhead out across the flight line and the hands away from the body. This could cause a badly pulled shot or a slice, or even a half-topped impact.

The proper start of the downswing begins with the *hips* rotating to the left quickly, followed by the turn of the shoulders to the left. This causes the hands and arms to move. (Hips make a slight lateral slide to the left before rotating.)

ITEMS 2 and 3. While the upper body must turn as described above, a premature complete turn causes "hitting from the top" with resulting loss of power.

Lead the club down with a strong pull of the left hand, with the top of the club's handle pointing toward the ground, and the wrists *still cocked.*

ITEMS 4, 5, and 6. Uncocking of the wrists too soon would lose much of the desired clubhead speed. When the hips move first, then the shoulders, then the hands and arms, the right elbow returns to the right side of the body. The wrists are still cocked at this point. When the right knee is thrust forward toward the target, just before uncocking the wrists, and with a *push off* the inside of the right foot, the clubhead is put into a strong hitting position, which releases the right side to follow the hit.

ITEMS 7 and 8. With the uncocking of the wrists, a split second before impact with the ball, the clubhead speed is increased to the maximum at the point of impact, through the release or uncocking of wrists being completed at the exact bottom of the downswing. This snaps them through the ball, with the right hand passing over the left in the process. Maximum distance in the hit is the natural result.

ITEM 9. Once again, keeping the head pretty still and both eyes on the ball prevents lunging or lateral sway to the left in the downswing, which could ruin the hit. If your entire swing has been correct, you won't need to look up to see where the ball is going. It will go straight and true, where you intended—and LONG!

Impact: For solid strikes, your left arm and the clubshaft should return to an "in-line" position.

STEP 4. IMPACT AND FOLLOW-THROUGH

What to Do

1. Just before impact with the ball, make sure that the *right* shoulder comes down and under the chin. This shoulder moves farther to the left than its position at address. The *left* shoulder rises.

2. At impact, the left arm is kept straight, and the right arm is slightly bent.

3. Hit "through" the ball, and not *at it.*

4. After impact, extend the arms as far as possible—with the follow-through *low,* and the weight shifted to the *inside* of the left foot at first.

5. Finish the follow-through on the *outside* of the left foot, with the body turned toward the target.

Follow-through: Hit through the ball, not at it. "Throw" the clubhead at the target. Extend both arms as far as possible, so the "toe" of the club points skyward.

Finish: To encourage a full and free move through the impact zone, try to finish with 95 percent of your weight on the outside of your left foot, and your belly button facing slightly left of target.

At this point, the *weight must be on the left foot,* with the *right* foot on the *toe,* merely steadying the body, and the right knee pointing toward the target.

Why You Do It

ITEM 1. As a preliminary to actual impact with the ball, one must be sure that the *right* shoulder comes down and under the chin just before the impact.

Actually, this shoulder at impact moves farther to the left than its original position at address. This assures that the body weight has properly shifted to the left, and that the *left* shoulder continues to rise throughout the impact and into the follow-through. This smooth forward and upward rise of the left shoulder automatically brings the right shoulder down and under as described above.

ITEM 2. During the actual impact, the left arm is *straight* to assure firmness in the hit, and to maintain good clubhead control. However, the *right* arm must be slightly *bent*. Should the right arm be straight at impact, power in the hit will be spent too rapidly.

The key to power in the hit, as well as accuracy, is the delayed wrist action, or uncocking of the wrists in the downswing, just before impact with the ball. This generally results from keeping the right elbow close to the body, and bringing the right shoulder down and under as the clubhead whips through at the ball.

The left hand must be the controlling and guiding element of the swing. If this hand is maintaining this control, however, one may hit as hard as possible with the right hand, provided it does not overpower the left. Should this happen, it is generally because the left hand is not keeping the proper control.

ITEM 3. After the impact, the right arm must immediately straighten in order to provide maximum acceleration of the clubhead.

The most important thing a player should have fixed in his mind on *all full shots* with every club is to make certain that he hits "through" the ball *fully,* rather than just *at* the ball. A smooth, full swing through the hitting area, "throwing" the clubhead at the target, will help to promote accuracy and provide good distance in the shot.

This enables the ball to "ride" on the clubface for a split second longer after the natural compression of the ball at impact, and the resulting recoil of compression after the hit. This is in sharp contrast to the ineffectual results of simply slapping at the ball and quitting on the follow-through.

ITEMS 4 and 5. A low follow-through, with fully extended arms, is evidence that the player has hit "through" the ball, and has shifted the weight to the left foot. Adequate body turn toward the target at the finish of the follow-through brings both hips around to a point at right angles to the target. The

weight must then rest mainly on the left foot, with the body being steadied by the toe of the right foot. The body will then be facing forward, and the right knee will also be pointing toward the target.

The head must stay behind the ball throughout the downswing, with the eyes maintained on the ball position until contact is made. As the follow-through takes place, and the body is forced around in a position facing the target, the head should turn slowly to the target as a result of the body turn. Don't be a "peeker" and look up too soon. There is plenty of time to see the ball's flight after the hit.

There you have it—the four vital steps of the basic swing, completely outlined, illustrated, and explained. Once you memorize the techniques in each step, and practice until your mind and body become accustomed to doing automatically what each step calls for, you can graduate to the "power-swing." But, before you try to employ that sophisticated action, designed to give you 10 to 20 extra yards off the tee, we suggest you do some exercises to increase your flexibility and prevent injuries to particular muscles.

PREVENTING GOLF INJURIES

What to Do

EXERCISE 1: Hamstring Stretch—Stand by a chair or bench and put one leg up on the support, straight with the knee locked. Cock the foot backward as you bend forward toward your knee (stretching the calf), then slowly lower the foot and feel the stretch move back into the hamstring. Only the foot moves in this exercise. Repeat five to seven times with each leg.

EXERCISE 2: Groin—Spread feet far apart with one leg locked and attempt to "sit" into opposite heel. Don't stretch too fast or past the point of pain. Release the stretch slowly, then "sit" into the opposite heel, cautiously. Follow a few stretches with six slow toe touches.

EXERCISE 3: Lower Back—Stand with the arms folded across the chest. Bend backward without strain, then to sides and forward. Do not strain. Repeat ten times daily.

THE POWER SWING

What to Do

ADDRESS: Line up everything square to the target line—feet, hips, and shoulders. Distribute your weight equally between the ball and heel of each foot.

Because you want to hit the ball high to carry it a long way, play the ball up in your stance, off your left instep, and set up with your head well behind the ball. This also puts you in the ideal position to take the club back naturally with your right hand.

Use the Vardon overlapping grip, but grip lightly. Too tight a grip will cause your muscles to get too tense and the clubhead speed will be too slow. It's like boxing. When a boxer's arm muscles are tense, he can hit hard, but his punch is slow. Relax, because clubhead speed is what hits the ball a long way.

THE TAKEAWAY. Let your right hand direct the backswing; use about 70 percent right hand to 30 percent left hand on the backswing. That will feel more natural simply because your right hand is probably the one you use most often in your daily life.

If you use your left hand too much in the backswing, your hips will tend to turn too early, and you will lose the coil of your upper body against the resistance of your legs.

By swinging back with your right hand, your hips stay secure; they don't turn prematurely. Your left knee automatically is pulled in toward the ball, and your right leg acts as a solid brace. In addition, a right-handed takeaway action encourages a long, powerful extension of the clubhead along the target line at the start—a "must" for creating a big swing arc.

THE TURN. Another vital secret to generating power is employing a huge shoulder turn. You get this by continuing to pull the club back and up with your right hand and arm on the backswing. At the top of your swing, in addition to turning your shoulders about 90 to 100 degrees, your left knee should be broken in behind the ball. Again, your right leg should be braced. This sets you up for a powerful movement with your legs through the ball on the downswing.

Even though you want a big shoulder turn, you want control, too. So don't let the club swing too far beyond the parallel position at the top. To encourage this, start moving your knees targetward the second you feel your weight fully shift to the "inside" of your right foot on the backswing.

THE DOWNSWING. Move your knees toward the target. Your coiled backswing sets you up for this. From your top-of-the-swing position, it's easy for you to use your legs on the downswing and avoid hitting from the top. Your swing to this point has set you up for a very late release of the hands, which is yet another link to power. And although your knees drive, your hips should start to turn to the left at the same time, to keep the club on the correct path and to generate more power.

The main elements here are moving the legs left and staying behind the ball with the head. If you used your left hand too much, you couldn't stay behind the ball very well. But, by using your right hand, you can stay behind the ball for that big "power play" in the impact zone.

2

The Fairway Woods

If you love the game as most golfers do, the study and practice of the techniques contained in this chapter will definitely prove worth your efforts. You will be surprised at the short time it takes to learn to make good clean shots from the fairway with your woods.

Before getting into the subject of your fairway woods shots, we suggest that you pay close attention to this chapter and read about what frequently happens to the player who takes no pregame warmup.

THE PREGAME WARMUP

How often has the average golfer stepped up to the first tee feeling that "this is his day," the day he is going to have one of his best rounds?

It is a beautiful day, with little or no wind. The other members of the foursome are fine companions, and a good competitive match has been arranged.

His drive is fairly good—not long, but straight down the fairway. As he strolls toward his ball, he is convinced that today he "really has it." Then something happens.

He has probably started out "cold," with no practice warmup. His body muscles are not yet tuned to the work they are being required to do, and what is perhaps worse, his superconfidence (while a good attitude) is far out of proportion to the other equally important requirement, *concentration.*

He forgets to concentrate on his second shot, and as a result it ends up only a few yards from where it was hit. Frustrated, he tries again, thinking more about the preceding poor shot than what he must do to recover, and the same thing happens again.

Now he begins to press, embarrassed because he feels he is letting his partners down, and you know the rest—he finishes the first hole with a triple bogey or worse. While there may be some improvement on the next 2 holes, his total score for the first 3 eliminates all chance of a good front 9 score.

Why let this happen, or at least why not try to prevent it by taking a good warmup before starting? Swinging a couple of clubs before starting will help, but 15 to 30 minutes on the practice range is the real solution. In this amount of time the body muscles have loosened, the need for concentration has been established, and you are ready.

Come out to the course a little ahead of your game time, use your practice range often—then watch your game improve.

THE FAIRWAY WOODS

You now have some idea of the necessity and scoring importance of pregame warmup, and the continuing value of *concentrating* on every shot played throughout a round of golf.

The all-important first 3 holes are those in which a good start is made, or they can become the nemesis to a good-scoring round.

So, too, can the last 3 holes. These come at a time when you are beginning to tire, particularly those who do not play often. The legs are tired, shoulders and muscles are getting stiff, and you begin to feel just a little older. So you begin to try harder and press, which can only result in overswinging, and getting off balance. Result, you miss some of your shots—most of them—and up goes your score for the second 9 holes.

When this happens, it is better to make your swing more compact, with a shorter backswing, and settle for a little less distance if necessary. With an easier swing and concentration on your remaining shots, the last 3 holes should not spoil your game.

Since the matter of obtaining distance in most of your fairway shots is an important part of good scoring, the use of fairway woods is essential for the average golfer. On all par 5 holes, as well as most long par 4 holes, a fairway wood of some kind is the required club to use if you expect to hit the green in the regulation number of strokes.

These woods are the *distance* clubs, and are called for when maximum distance is required and the lie of the ball or the elements does not force you to consider an iron instead.

The most vital backswing key on fairway wood shots is sweeping the clubhead low to the turf in the takeaway.

HIT HARD FOR DISTANCE

Before getting into the subject of which of the fairway woods to use, and how to use them, there are several important points to keep in mind:

1. Correct ball position.
2. Swing smoothly, and keep your balance. Keep your eyes on the ball.
3. Hit *hard*, but don't *lunge.*
4. Follow through *completely.*

NO. 3 WOOD

What to Do

1. Line up your next shot as you approach your ball.

The most vital downswing key on fairway wood shots is sweeping the clubhead through the ball.

2. If your ball is sitting down slightly in fairway grass, and if you have any doubt that it can be hit cleanly with a driver, use the No. 3 wood.

3. Since the shaft is shorter for the No. 3 wood than for the driver, stand slightly closer to the ball.

4. At address, the clubhead should be set *flat* on the ground in its natural lie, so as not to distort the loft of the club.

5. For the No. 3 wood, the ball should be played a few inches to the right of the left heel.

6. On the downswing, the clubface is brought into the ball *before* it has reached the bottom of the swing arc. A very shallow turf divot will, therefore, be taken after the ball has been hit off a tight fairway.

7. See the shot come to life in your mind's eye before triggering your backswing.

8. Don't try to "punch" down so hard that you end up with too large a divot, and no distance to your shot.

9. Use the same smooth and complete follow-through as for all full shots.

In addressing a fairway wood, always sole the clubhead flush to the grass and set the clubface squarely to both the ball and target.

How to Do It

Since the shaft is shorter for the No. 3 wood than for the driver, put yourself in the "control position" by standing slightly closer to the ball as the player has done here.

On fairway wood shots, don't ever open the face drastically in an attempt to help the ball up.

On fairway wood shots, don't ever close the face drastically in an attempt to help the ball up.

ITEMS 5, 6, and 7. Playing the ball a few inches to the right of the left heel for a No. 3 wood shot (on a level lie) will bring the clubhead into the ball just *before* the bottom of the swing arc has been reached. The ball is hit first, with a divot taken after the impact. Visualizing a fine shot at address sends a positive message to the brain. And confidence is vital to consistently hitting woods crisply and accurately.

ITEM 8. The player should guard against "punching" down so abruptly that he "bloops" the shot high and for only a short distance. Hitting the ball *before* the bottom of the swing arc has been reached is sufficient to create the condition of "hitting down" at the ball. It is not necessary to punch down excessively to assure getting the ball up in the air.

ITEM 9. For shots from a *level* lie, with a No. 3 wood, it's important that the player preserve his timing and keep his swing smooth and compact. Hit *through* the ball, and don't punch *at* it. Follow through completely, and finish the swing with the hands high.

Why You Do It

ITEM 1. Once again, as you approach your ball after having made your tee shot, or for a par 5 hole, when you are hitting to the green, give consideration to the things necessary to attain your objective. Don't wait until you have reached your ball to start thinking of these things.

ITEM 2. The No. 3 wood is the safest club to use in order to get the ball up and winging, and to attain the maximum distance possible. This is assuming a shorter and more lofted wood club is not the better choice because of a following wind, or the distance to target being less than that which would require a longer wood club.

ITEMS 3 and 4. Since the No. 3 wood shaft is shorter than the driver's shaft, the swing arc is therefore somewhat less. The player should stand closer to the ball for this shot, and the stance will be correct when addressing the ball if the clubhead is resting *flat* on its sole.

On No. 3 wood shots, the club should swing "inside" the target line on the backswing.

For best results on No. 3 wood shots, keep the backswing controlled. Swing within yourself.

3. BECAUSE OF THE SHORTER SHAFT, STAND CLOSER TO THE BALL THAN FOR LONGER CLUBS. MAKE SURE TO SOLE THE CLUBHEAD ON THE GROUND AT ADDRESS.

4. POSITION THE BALL MIDWAY BETWEEN THE LEFT HEEL AND THE CENTER OF THE STANCE FOR NORMAL LIES.

5. USE THE SAME "ONE-PIECE" SWING AS FOR ALL FULL SHOTS.

6. KEEP THE HEAD STILL, EYES ON THE BALL, THROUGHOUT THE COMPLETE SWING.

7. FOLLOW THROUGH *low* and *fully* as for all full swings.

8. Be sure to finish the swing with the weight on the left foot.

How to Do It

The No. 4 wood is an excellent tool for hitting the fairway bunker shot, provided you stand with your feet flat on the sand.

NO. 4 WOOD

What to Do

1. Check your lie and intended course of action as you approach your ball.

2. The No. 4 wood is the club to use when good distance is required, and the following obstacles must be overcome:

   A. When the ball rests in fairly deep rough off the fairway, and is a good distance from the target.
   B. When the ball is sitting up well in a fairway bunker, and the forward lip of the bunker can be easily cleared. *Hit the ball cleanly.*
   C. When there is a tree along the target line, about 50–75 yards in front of your ball, and a successful shot with a long iron is doubtful.

When hitting a No. 4 wood out of a bunker, don't ever dig your feet in too deeply; otherwise you will restrict your body turn and, thus, lose power.

Why You Do It

ITEM 1. Determining your course of action as you approach your ball for the next shot saves the necessity for filling your mind with these things after you take your stance. Besides, it speeds up play on the course.

One of the real great professional tournament players was asked how he could hit so quickly when he reached his ball. His answer was, "I have already figured out what I must do before I have reached my ball, and the fewer things I have to think about while preparing to execute my shot, the more *relaxed* and *positive* I can be, so I just go ahead and hit."

He further stated that "anyone who stands over his ball longer than *five seconds* is beginning to doubt himself."

Concentration is necessary, but the longer one deliberates before making his shot, the more chance that the subconscious will become filled with dis-

turbing elements which could make one too tense, and spoil the shot execution. So, once you have lined up your stance with the club you have decided to use, go ahead and hit.

ITEM 2A. When the ball is buried deep in the fairway turf, or in a deep divot, the No. 4 wood with its more lofted clubface is the club to use. The loss of distance between this club and the longer fairway woods is negligible.

ITEM 2B. To use the No. 4 wood from fairly deep rough is all right provided the ball is not buried in very heavy grass or leafy weeds. For this condition, a more lofted short iron may be better, since the heavy growth may slow down the clubhead too much, or even divert its direction. With a slight adjustment in the swing, however, wherein the player hits down sharply at the ball (which is played more toward the *center* of the stance), one can nearly always attain more distance with a No. 4 wood than by using a long iron, much less a short one.

ITEM 2C. When good distance to the target is required, and the ball is "sitting up" well in a fairway bunker, the No. 4 wood is an excellent club to use, provided the forward lip of the bunker is low enough to be cleared. The ball *must be hit cleanly,* taking *no sand.* Don't ground the clubhead in the trap. It is against the rules.

ITEM 2D. When there is a tree in front of the line to the target, the extra loft of the No. 4 wood *usually* will clear the tree, provided the ball is far enough back from the tree to gain the height of flight necessary for clearance. When in doubt, use a long iron, and "punch" out to a safe position. Don't gamble and waste a stroke.

ITEM 3. Using the No. 4 wood, stand even closer to the ball than for the No. 3 wood, because the shaft is a little shorter. The proper position of the stance is again determined by placing the sole of the clubhead *flat* on the ground, and with the stance and body position the same as for other wood clubs.

ITEMS 4 and 5. Positioning the ball midway between the left heel and the center of the stance, for normal lies, assures that the ball will be hit *before* the bottom of the downswing arc has been reached. Make sure that the swing is smooth and compact, and that the clubhead is not punched down into the ground. The ball position will take care of the hit down into the ball.

ITEM 6. As for all shots, keep the *head still, eyes on the ball,* until well *after* the hit. Moving the head can cause a "fat" hit, and looking up can cause a topped shot.

ITEMS 7 and 8. A smooth, well-timed hit *through* the ball is essential for good distance. It is the same for all full shots. *Lunging* at the ball, or flipping the clubhead *at* it, can never achieve the distance and straight flight to the target which are the desired objectives. Again, finish the swing with the weight on the left foot, and the hands high.

TAILORING THE TIP

For most players, the Nos. 1, 3, and 4 woods are the most popular and generally used wood clubs. But there are even more lofted wood clubs than these—particularly the No. 5 wood—that many players find of real value in reaching their objectives.

These "utility woods" have a certain value under extreme conditions, particularly when playing a shot off a steep downhill lie, or out of heavy rough where more distance is needed than can be expected from a short iron.

There is a definite place for such clubs in the typical amateur's bag, however, particularly for the woman golfer, whose iron shots may not give her the distance she feels she can obtain from the higher lofted woods.

We strongly recommend the No. 5 wood for women players. Also we definitely recommend that golfers who have an average score of 90 or over discard the No. 2 iron and replace it with a No. 5 wood.

Your pro shop is bound to carry a wide assortment of No. 5 woods for you to choose from, and your professional instructor will be glad to advise you on the proper technique.

A NOTE TO WOMEN GOLFERS

Mastering the woods is one key to better golf for the average woman golfer, simply because the typi-

cal female player hits one or more wood shots on almost every hole, including approach shots on par-4s and tee shots on par-3s.

It's important to understand that a wooden clubhead is specially designed to hit the ball into the air. Therefore, there's no need to try and help it up by attempting to scoop it off the grass. Swing the club through the hitting area smoothly and make good contact with the ball, and the clubhead will do the work.

The next fundamental for good wood play is that you must swing the club with a sweeping action through impact, rather than hitting with a sharp, descending blow. A sweeping or "brushing" action will provide the squarest and most solid contact with the ball, creating power by efficiently transmitting clubhead speed.

To create this action, start with a sound grip. For many women, a stronger grip, with both hands turned more to the right on the club, will help them control the club with the left arm, promoting a swinging of the arms, instead of a lifting with the hands.

A strong address position, with good posture, is also important. Stand to the ball with a slight bend at the waist, a slight flex at the knees, and balanced weight distribution. You'll then be in the perfect position to swing your arms freely and use your lower body effectively during the swing. The width of your stance is also an important point. Many women use a stance that is far too narrow. A shoulder-width stance is ideal for playing the driver and fairway woods. This is narrow enough to provide ease of movement, but wide enough to give you a solid foundation.

Start the backswing by sweeping the club away low and straight back from the ball for the first 18 inches. A one-piece takeaway, arms, shoulders, and hips starting back simultaneously, will trigger a full turn of the body on the backswing. A full turn winds up the torso muscles for power and helps to create a positive weight shift to the right, while allowing you to set the club in a solid position at the top of the swing.

In starting the downswing, you may benefit by thinking of shifting the weight to the left side while turning the hips back toward the target. Leading with the lower body puts the movements of the downswing in the correct sequence, with the arms folding naturally.

Through the hitting zone, give the ball a good whack with a free swing of the arms. This increases your power and accuracy through improved squaring of the clubface.

The last important point in the swing is the follow-through. You'll rarely see a strong wood player with a short or cramped follow-through. Swinging through to a high, full finish will help you to accelerate the club through the hitting zone. And rather than stunting the follow-through by keeping your head rigidly down, allow your head to come up with your right shoulder as you swing through.

THE DOWNHILL
NO. 3 WOOD SHOT

What to Do

Ordinarily, the correct ball position for a fairway wood shot is just inside the left heel. From a steep downhill lie, however, you want to move it back

about 3 inches, just ahead of center, and stand wider than normal. Kick your right knee in slightly and let it carry most of your weight at address.

Choke down slightly on the grip and swing back no further than the three-quarter position.

On the downswing, you must swing the clubhead through the ball and extend it down the slope, with your weight shifting well onto your left side. You've got to stay with this shot longer than any other and trust the loft of the club to get the ball up.

The number-one downswing key on downhill No. 5 wood shots is to swing down the slope.

In hitting a downhill No. 5 wood shot, you must play the ball back in your stance.

3
Iron Play

Many players, particularly the older ones, whose tee shots are somewhat shorter than those of their playing companions, have learned to become so accurate with their iron shots that they are consistently able to hit the ball close to the flagstick for an easy par or even a birdie, while their longer-hitting friends are spraying their slugged shots in all directions.

Accordingly, the more time you can give to the *study* and *practice* of the following pages on the science of *iron play,* the sooner you will find yourself listed in the low handicap bracket. Iron clubs are designed more for accuracy than for long distance. A good golfer, therefore, finesses. He carefully plans out each iron shot, sticks to a set pre-swing routine, and swings smoothly, using only 80 to 85 percent of his power to propel the ball targetward.

The Nos. 2, 3, and 4 irons are called the long irons, and are the ones to use when the lie on the fairway does not permit the use of a wood club, although a maximum distance is required. Also, under windy conditions it is far safer to use a long iron than a wood club such as the No. 3 or No. 4.

The middle irons (Nos. 5 and 6) and the short clubs (Nos. 7 to 9 and both wedges) are the ones which help you to send your ball straight to the flagstick, within easy putting distance. Accuracy with these clubs helps many players, particularly older ones, to score well, though they may not be able to hit the greens in regulation strokes.

Every golfer should learn his own distance capabilities for each iron club under all conditions. To start with, it is a good idea for him to use at least one number lower than he thinks for various distances, particularly where a full shot is required.

The following chart shows the average distances for male players expected under normal conditions. Check your own distances for each club, and record them in the space provided below. Then choose the club that will send your ball to the target without having to force the shot.

CLUB USED	AVERAGE DISTANCE	YOUR DISTANCE
No. 1 Wood	220 Yards	———
No. 3 Wood	200 "	———
No. 4 Wood	190 "	———
No. 5 Wood	185 "	———
No. 2 Iron	180 "	———
No. 3 Iron	170 "	———
No. 4 Iron	160 "	———
No. 5 Iron	150 "	———
No. 6 Iron	140 "	———
No. 7 Iron	130 "	———
No. 8 Iron	120 "	———
No. 9 Iron	110 "	———
P.W.	100 "	———
S.W.	80 "	———

A FOOLPROOF PRESHOT ROUTINE

What to Do

To become a consistently good iron player, you must develop a fixed routine for taking your address position. A routine helps you make sure that all the fundamentals are correct before you swing, and also keeps you in motion so that your muscles remain relaxed but ready to move.

What follows is a suggested routine including elements used by the top professionals.

Step 1. Stand behind the ball, looking toward the target. Fix the target line in your mind. If you prefer sighting along a spot on the target line rather than the line itself, pick a spot in front of the ball, such as a clump of discolored grass.

Step 2. Step into the "golfer's box" from the side—right foot first—and keep focusing on the target to form a strong mental picture of the shot you plan to play.

Step 3. Bring your left foot up to your right and put your feet together, with the ball centered between them. This move makes it easy for you to spread your feet parallel to the target line.

Step 4. Move your left foot to the left, positioning the ball in the correct position in relation to the left heel. Then move your right foot to the right, to the correct width of the stance.

Step 5. To relax any tension, waggle the club.

Step 6. Set the club squarely behind the ball, then start your backswing.

THE LONG IRONS

These clubs are perhaps the most difficult ones, and to master them requires study and practice—and lots of it.

You must develop confidence in your ability to use them, and this can only come from a thorough knowledge of the fundamentals, and then practicing until things begin to fall into place.

What to Do

1. While approaching the ball in the fairway, determine all things necessary—the lie, impeding hazards, wind direction, club to use, etc. If a long iron is chosen:

   A. Take the stance with the basic form as for wood clubs.
   B. Stand closer to the ball.
   C. Grip the club firmly (since the shock of hitting the turf with the clubface might cause it to turn in the player's hands, if the grip, particularly with the left hand, is too loose).
   D. A square stance is preferred for long iron shots, with feet spread not quite as wide as for wood shots. This allows a full backswing and pivot, with full turn of the shoulders to the right.
   E. Play the ball from a position in which it can be hit cleanly—usually slightly to the right of the instep or heel of the left foot.

2. START THE BACKSWING *(low* and *slow)* with fully extended arms, until the hands reach hip height, then cock the wrists.

3. With the stance closer to the ball, the backswing is slightly more upright than for wood clubs. (This is a further aid to accuracy.)

4. At the top of the backswing, the hands are not brought much higher than the shoulders.

5. The downswing is started in the same manner as with the wood clubs, although the swing arc is slightly more vertical.

6. Keep the entire swing in one piece, and do not allow the head or body to sway.

7. The weight shifts to the left on the downswing, with the majority of the weight on the inside of the left foot just before impact with the ball.

8. At impact, the back of the left hand and the palm of the right hand should be *square* to the line of flight.

9. Follow through low, with the right arm fully extended. Finish with the hands high and 95 percent of the weight on the outside of the left foot.

How to Do It

Make a one-piece takeaway and extend your arms back, so the toe of the club points skyward.

On long irons, set your feet, knees, hips, and shoulders square to the target, but move closer to the ball than on wood shots, to promote control.

Employ a strong shoulder turn going back. To encourage this action, rotate your left shoulder under your chin.

The secret of the follow-through is extending the arms targetward so the toe of the club returns to a skyward position.

At the start of the downswing, pull the club downward with your hands and feel the weight shift over to your left side.

At impact, the back of your left hand and the palm of your right hand should be square to the target.

Finish with your left hip cleared to the left, the majority of your weight on the outside of your left foot, and your hands high.

To groove a good sweeping action with long irons, try to brush a forward tee with the clubhead, through impact.

Why You Do It

ITEM 1. This item should be self-explanatory, so concentrate on your course of action for your next shot before you arrive at your ball's position in the fairway.

ITEMS 1A and 1B. The stance is the same as for wood shots, except slightly closer to the ball, since the clubshafts are somewhat shorter. Make sure that the hands are slightly *ahead* of the ball at address, and that *clubshaft, hands,* and *arms* form a *straight line* from the left shoulder to the ball.

ITEM 1C. A loose grip with the left hand will invariably cause the clubface to "open up" with the shock of impact with the ball and ground. A sliced shot is the natural result. Grip firmly with the left hand, and make sure that *both* hands are closely "welded" together.

ITEM 1D. For older players who have difficulty making a full shoulder turn to the right in the backswing a slightly closed stance will help. Be sure, however, that the right foot is placed only a *few inches* back of the left in relation to the line of flight.

ITEM 1E. Playing the ball off the left heel, or slightly to the right of this point, assures hitting it at the *bottom* of the swing arc. While this gives the effect of hitting the ball a downward blow, actually in most instances you "sweep" the ball off the turf with the *long* irons.

ITEM 2. The most important phase of the swing with the long irons, as with most clubs, is the first 12 inches of the start of the backswing. Keeping the clubhead low to the ground for this distance in the takeaway from the ball, and with fully extended arms, until the hands reach hip height, prevents picking up the clubhead sharply, and sets up a good body pivot.

ITEM 3. Since the shafts of iron clubs become progressively shorter as the loft of the clubface increases, the swing arc becomes shorter and more upright.

ITEM 4. While it is true that the higher the hands are brought in the backswing, with the woods and long irons, the more power can be generated in the downswing, it is best for the average player to keep his swing *compact* and within his personal limits. Iron shots are made for accuracy more than for extra distance. You should not slug with irons. In fact, the swing for the long irons should be no harder than for *full* shots with the shorter irons.

ITEMS 5 and 6. Don't rush the backswing or downswing with the long irons. Keep it smooth, and in one piece. Above all, keep the head as still as possible, and don't lunge at the ball. Also, don't crouch too much in addressing the ball. Stand tall, with only a slight flexing of the knees.

ITEM 7. With the hip turn to the left becoming the start of the downswing, the body weight automatically shifts to the left foot. Actually, the first move of the hips is slightly lateral (without body sway), followed by the turn of the hips as the weight shifts.

ITEM 8. At impact with the ball, the left arm *must*

be in control, to guide the clubhead *through* the ball and out toward the target. The back of the left hand and the palm of the right hand *must* face the target also. Rolling the wrists to the left causes a badly pulled shot.

ITEM 9. As for all full shots, follow through low with arms fully extended, particularly the right, until the hands raise naturally to a high finish. "Throw" the clubhead out toward the target after the hit.

THE MIDDLE IRONS

What to Do

1. When approaching the ball, mentally size up the situation and determine the things to do: distance to the flagstick on the green, club to use, etc.

2. Where a middle iron is indicated, select a club of sufficient length for the distance required, based upon your personal ability. *(When in doubt, use at least one club longer.)*

3. The stance is slightly closer to the ball than for long irons, and is slightly more open.

4. The ball is positioned a few inches back of a line even with the left heel. In other words, more toward the center of the stance. The hands should be ahead of the ball.

5. The backswing is the same as for long irons *(low* and *slow),* with both arms fully extended until the hands reach hip height.

6. At this point the wrists break, with the left arm kept comfortably straight.

7. In pivoting to the right, keep the knees fairly level instead of dipping the left knee (as for the longer club shots). The left heel is lifted only enough to make the action of the pivot comfortable, with slight pressure off the inside of the left foot.

8. At the top of the backswing, see that the head

is *still* over the ball, and that a firm grip is kept on the club's handle.

9. Start the downswing the same as for the long irons, with the left hip leading the turn to the left, and the left foot coming down flat on the ground in a "sitting down" to the ball action.

10. The wrists remain cocked until they are slightly below the hips, when they start to uncock with a snap.

11. Strike the ball a descending blow, taking a divot after impact. Keep your eyes on the ball until well after impact.

12. Follow through low with fully extended arms, and with the weight finishing on the left foot.

How to Do It

On middle iron shots, your stance should be a bit narrower and slightly closer to the ball than for long irons, since the swing should be more upright.

Swing back on a narrower arc and keep the action under control by not allowing the clubhead to swing past the parallel position.

To groove a good arms-swing with the medium irons, employ a smooth backswing action with your feet together. Then pause.

To ensure good bodily balance, which is a must for achieving clean, crisp clubface-to-ball contact, keep your knees flexed through impact.

Why You Do It

ITEM 1. When the lie of the ball is close enough to the green to require only a middle or short iron shot, it is doubly important to mentally determine the strategy for the shot to the target as you approach the ball. When you start to *execute* the shot, only one thing should be uppermost in your mind —hitting the ball as close to the flagstick as possible. Everything else should already have been decided.

ITEM 2. Know *your own distances* for each club, through *practice.* Considering such factors as wind direction, condition and position of the green, etc., use the club that will propel the ball all the way to your target. For most golfers (not professionals) their shots are more often *short* of the target than past it. If you can hit your ball close to the flagstick, it *might* go in the cup, or at least end up close enough for a short putt. If you are consistently short with your shots, you lose both ways.

ITEMS 3 and 4. The shafts for the middle irons are even shorter than those of the long irons, so the stance is naturally closer to the ball. Also, since the swing arc is shorter and more compact, the stance becomes more open as the shorter irons are used. The ball being positioned a few inches to the right of the left heel permits the impact to occur *before* the bottom of the swing arc is reached. A divot is therefore taken after the ball is struck. With the hands slightly ahead of the clubhead, a properly lofted shot is assured, assuming the entire swing is well executed.

ITEMS 5 and 6. Keep the backswing smooth and unhurried, with the left arm and clubshaft forming a straight line. Don't let the clubhead lag behind the hands during the takeaway, or catch on the grass during this process by grounding the club too firmly on the turf.

When the clubhead reaches approximately hip height, the wrists should break automatically, but this should be kept at a minimum. Keep the entire backswing smooth and in one piece, with the left arm comfortably straight throughout the swing.

ITEM 7. Since the middle and short irons are played more for accuracy than for distance, the body and shoulder turn become less, and the backswing more upright. Therefore, the knees remain fairly level,

To get in the groove of swishing the club through at a relatively high speed, keep your feet together and swing through the ball.

with very little lifting of the left heel during the pivot to the right.

Of the greatest importance is making sure that the *right* shoulder is *lower* than the left at address, and at the start of the backswing. The low right shoulder makes it easy to keep the right arm "hinged" and tucked in close to the right side for the start of a smooth backswing.

ITEM 8. Keep the head still, with both eyes on the ball. Fat hits are generally attributed to head movement and body sway. Part of this is frequently due to the player trying to slug the ball with too short a club for the distance required. In an effort to gain extra power in the hit, he stretches his backswing too far, causing head and body movement to the right. If in the process he also loosens the grip on the club's handle, the clubface alignment is changed, and only a miracle could allow him to regrip for a square clubface at impact.

ITEMS 9 and 10. The downswing for the middle irons starts with the left hip leading, followed by the turn of the shoulders. The arms are drawn downward, with the wrists still cocked until the hands are just below the hips. The tip of the club handle should then be pointing toward the ground, and the right elbow brought in close to the right front of the body. This is the start of the "uncoiling" of the right side muscles.

When the right side (hip, shoulder, and leg) is relaxed, and moves around to the target line, and the left side firms up, the weight shifts to the left foot, setting up a "wall of resistance" anchored in the left heel. As the wrists uncock with a snap, the clubhead speed increases naturally, providing all the power necessary. Keep the swing "lazy" and fluid.

ITEMS 11 and 12. Since the swing for the middle irons is more upright than for longer clubs, and impact with the ball is just *before* the bottom of the swing arc has been reached, a divot will be taken after impact with the ball. Hit the back of the ball *first;* the divot-taking follows. This points up the importance of keeping the head still and the eyes on the ball until well after impact. Otherwise, a fat hit or top could result.

Following through low with fully extended arms will assure hitting *through* the ball instead of *at* it. It also assures shifting the weight fully to the left side. Finishing with the hands high indicates that all parts of the swing have been correct, with a good turn and tilt of the shoulders. It also assures getting the maximum distance from the hit, and helps promote accuracy of the ball's flight.

THE SHORT IRONS

Full Shots

HIT THE TARGET

Because of the extreme importance the short iron clubs play in a good score, when playing *full shots* with these clubs we believe the following points should be stressed before outlining the complete techniques in making these shots:

1. Don't underclub yourself. If in doubt, use one *more* club.

2. Don't overswing. The objective is *accuracy,* not extra distance.

3. Follow through *low,* and finish with the clubhead pointing to the target.

What to Do

1. Mentally review the necessary course of action as you approach your ball.

2. Line up your shot to the target, and determine the club to use.

3. Take an open stance, with weight even on both *heels and soles* of both feet. Don't lean forward on the soles alone.

4. The position of the ball should be more toward the center of the stance, which will be closer to the ball than for either the long or the middle iron shots. The hands should be *ahead* of the clubhead at address.

5. Use very little body turn. Both feet should be kept on the ground throughout the backswing. Sixty percent of the weight should be on the *left* foot.

6. Take the club back *low* and *slow,* with a straight left arm. Use very little hip turn, but a full shoulder turn, until the chin touches the left shoulder.

7. The right elbow stays close to the body. Cock the wrists when the hands reach hip height.

8. The short iron swing is very upright.

9. Stretch the left arm to the full extent of your ability without straining, the same as for other iron shots.

10. On the downswing, the left shoulder moves away from the chin, bringing the club down to the ball. At this point, the left leg begins to brace, and by bracing we do not mean "locking" the left leg. Keep the swing fluid throughout.

11. The wrists begin to uncock at approximately hip height, snapping the clubhead down to the ball.

12. Stay *down to the ball.* Don't lift the left shoulder until well after impact.

13. Keep the left side firm to hit against, with the right arm slightly bent just before impact, and with the palm of the right hand *facing* the target. The right arm straightens after impact.

14. Hit down sharply on the ball, and then follow through (low and full), with the clubhead pointing toward the target.

How to Do It

A square stance: the "wrong" setup for short irons.

An open stance: the "right" setup for short irons.

On the backswing, your left shoulder should move toward your chin.

On the downswing, your left shoulder should move away
from your chin.

Keep your head behind the ball as you pull the club downward.

To promote a sharp downward hit of the club on the ball, practice hitting short irons from bad lies.

Why You Do It

ITEM 1. As the player comes closer to the green or target area, the accuracy of his shots becomes vitally important. Here is where the player who often does not hit the greens in the regulation number of strokes can overcome this problem and score well, *if* he can hit his ball to a point close to the flagstick for one putt. So it behooves him to plan his strategy carefully—i.e., the club to use, impeding hazards such as sand traps, trees, the slope of the green, etc. If you want to score well, this is the place to concentrate on the proper course of action.

ITEM 2. After lining up your shot to the target, make sure that your address position is also lined up correctly. If you are facing out of line with the intended flight direction, you can't expect the ball to go where you want.

ITEM 3. With the shorter irons, the backswing is shorter and more upright. An open stance is employed, therefore, with the left foot drawn back slightly from the intended line of flight.

ITEM 4. The ball must be struck with a firm downward stroke, and a divot taken, so the ball should be positioned toward the center of the stance. Since the shafts are shorter than those of middle and long irons, the stance is naturally closer to the ball. Correct address position finds the body inclined only a little, with the sole of the clubhead *flat* on the ground behind the ball. The hands should also be *ahead* of the clubhead, with the left arm and clubshaft forming a straight line to the left shoulder.

ITEM 5. Both feet remain on the ground throughout the backswing, with the weight resting mainly on the left foot. Since the backswing is more upright, there is very little body turn.

ITEMS 6 and 7. As for all full shots, the backswing is started by a push through the left arm, which is kept straight throughout the swing. For the shorter iron shots there is very little hip turn, but a *full* shoulder turn. The right elbow staying close to the body controls the plane of the backswing, and keeps the clubhead in proper alignment. Wrist-cocking takes place at approximately hip height, but is kept to a minimum of wrist break. Keep the swing in one piece.

ITEM 8. Taking the clubhead back low to the ground at the start of the backswing, with a straight left arm and proper shoulder turn, will assure taking it back inside the line of flight. Don't pick up the club sharply.

ITEM 9. Since most shots with a short iron are full shots involving a full backswing, the left arm should take the clubhead back as far as possible without straining. If the proper club has been selected for the distance required, the loft of the clubhead will prevent overshooting the target.

ITEM 10. At the start of the downswing, with the left shoulder moving away from the chin, the arms are again drawn down with the wrists still cocked. The full weight is then placed upon the left foot with the left leg beginning to brace, but not lock.

ITEMS 11 and 12. The delayed uncocking of the wrists again provides the increased clubhead speed to provide the proper power for the hit. *Stay down to the ball*—don't lift the left shoulder trying to "scoop" the ball up. After impact, the left shoulder will rise naturally.

ITEM 13. When the left side collapses instead of bracing, the left arm loses control and anything can happen, usually a badly pulled shot, or even a bad slice. The left arm should throw the clubhead out toward the target, with the palm of the right hand also facing this objective during impact. Keeping a firm left side throughout the downswing not only aids the flight direction but forces the right shoulder down, and brings the body in behind the shot for the required power.

ITEM 14. Hitting down sharply with a divot taken *after* the impact imparts backspin on the ball. The low and full follow-through, with the clubhead pointing toward the target after impact, helps to assure a straight shot and the attainment of the required distance.

GETTING THE BALL TO "SIT"— THE EASY WAY

1. Play the ball back in your stance.

2. Make a one-piece takeaway using minimal wrist cock.

3. Continue to swing the club back until you feel most of your weight shift to the inside of your right foot.

4. Allow your wrists to cock slightly, then swing the club straight up with your hands and arms.

5. To prevent getting out of the upright position swing the club back no farther than the three-quarter point.

6. Pull the club down with your hands and arms and hit down on the ball, trapping it against the clubface. It's this action that gets the ball to "sit" on the green.

TAILORING THE TIP

With the ball played back, you will make contact before the blade squares up to the intended target. The clubface will be a little open at impact, so the ball will fly a little left to right. To compensate for this fade action, aim slightly to the left of the target.

THE "FLIER": GOLF'S KILLER LIE

What to Do

Recovery Power

Most rough lies fit into the flier category, where the grass grows above the equator of the ball. In such course circumstances, grass will intervene between the ball and clubface at impact, which reduces spin and causes the ball to fly up to 20 yards farther in the air than normal. So, allow for this by taking at least one club less than what you would usually use for the required distance—i.e., a No. 8 iron, instead of a No. 7.

Whichever club you choose to play, you still will need a more upright backswing arc with a faster wrist break, because you have to deliver a sharp, downward blow to the ball to pop it out of the grass. Three adjustments in your normal address are necessary: 1. Play the ball back in your stance. 2. Open your stance slightly. 3. Don't ground the club (to avoid snagging it in the grass on the takeaway, which could destroy your timing).

The classic "flier" lie.

To promote a direct blow of the club on the ball, swing back on a very narrow arc.

THE ONE-QUARTER, HALF, AND THREE-QUARTER SWINGS

THREE COMMON COURSE SITUATIONS

What to Do

SITUATION 1: Good lie in the fairway. Hole is cut close to the green's edge, behind a bunker with a relatively low lip. You're 25 yards from the pin.

SHOT: One-quarter "scurrier" with a No. 5 iron.

TECHNIQUE: Put 60 percent of your weight on the left foot. Keep your lower body "quiet" as you swing the club back to the one-quarter position (hands at waist height) with very little wrist cock.

In the downswing, drive both knees toward the target and pull the clubface into the back of the ball. Mirror the one-quarter position at the finish.

The ball flies low, running through the trap over the lip. Slowed down by sand and fringe, the ball "dies" as it rolls toward the hole.

SITUATION 2: Ball sitting up in the fairway grass. You're hitting to a flag 110 yards away, cut on the top tier of a fast green.

SHOT: Half-swing "bouncer" with a No. 7 iron.

TECHNIQUE: Leave most of your weight on the left foot. Keep your left arm straight as you swing up to the halfway position (hands at chest height). Your left foot should stay planted throughout the swing to prevent swaying.

Pull the club down with your hands and arms. Finish the swing in the mirror image of the halfway position, hands at chest height, with your stomach facing the target.

The ball hits on the front of the green, bounces once or twice, and rolls toward the flag.

SITUATION 3: Excellent lie in the fairway. Ball is 140 yards from green, and a 20-mile-an-hour wind is in your face. There are no hazards in front of the green.

SHOT: Three-quarter "punch" with a No. 4 iron.

TECHNIQUE: Look down at the ball with your left eye. Make a smooth one-piece takeaway and, while turning your hips and shoulders and activating your knees, swing the club up to the three-quarter position (hands at head height).

At the start of the downswing, grip the club more tightly with both hands. You want to delay the release and drive the clubhead at the target, so keep your head down through impact.

Swing the club through to the three-quarter position. The ball pierces the wind and finishes on the green.

4

The Short Game

This section covers the part of golf which most players agree is the most important. Certainly, the ability to master the *short* game will contribute the most toward good scoring.

Many players, particularly men, are capable of hitting good, long drives off the tee. They may also hit most of their shots very well from the fairway. But if they don't hit the greens in the regulation number of strokes, they will certainly be called upon to make short pitch shots, chips, or even the more difficult shots from a sand trap. Then comes that part of the game which accounts for one half or more of all the strokes made in a total round of golf, *putting*.

The typical woman golfer is frequently able to develop her short game to the point where she can overcome the loss of distance from her drives, or fairway woods and iron shots. Result: She is able to score well. This also applies to many older players, whose strength and suppleness of body have dwindled a little, so that they too must sacrifice some distance in their shots with the longer clubs.

Because of our intense desire to help all students of the game, we urge everyone to *study* this section carefully, and *practice* religiously until these all-important phases have been mastered.

We all know how many times we have made a good long drive off the tee, another straight second shot (just short of the green), and then for some reason the pitch to the green is either too short or too long, and we end up taking 3 putts to get the ball in the cup. Hasn't this happened to you?

From the pitch shot to putting the ball in the cup, 4 shots have been made, *twice* as many as it took to get from the tee to the near edge of the green. For a par 4 hole this means a double bogey. Have too many of these and your score is ruined.

If you can learn to pitch and chip the ball reasonably close to the flagstick, you stand a good chance of dropping the ball for a par score. On the shorter par 4 holes, and most of the par 5 holes, a well-placed pitch shot, close to the flagstick, affords the player an opportunity to birdie the hole.

One of the surest ways to improve your pitching and chipping ability is to practice shots from various distances to a target. From such practice it is soon possible to learn the range for each club used, and get an idea as to the length of the backswing necessary for the needed distance. Of course, the first step is to have your teaching professional instruct you in proper form and technique.

Cut shots are more difficult, and perhaps should be practiced more often than the standard pitches or chips. These are valuable shots in hitting over trees, out of heavy rough or sand, or to pitch over a trap where there is little room for the ball to run on the green to the cup.

Playing out of sand traps is a harrowing experience for most high handicap players, and is the place where more shots are wasted than any other place on the golf course, except perhaps on the putting green. Even though these trap shots are more difficult for the average player than some others, they can be learned when one develops the proper coordination of mind, muscles, and nerves, which controls perfect timing.

Finally, good pitch shots, chips, and sand trap play will be of little consequence if one cannot putt the ball into the cup with reasonable regularity. With proper initial professional instruction, and a little regular practice, *anyone* can learn to putt well.

This section attempts to cover the basic principles of the various golf shots involved in the short game. Proficiency in their execution is necessary for good scoring.

THE PITCH SHOT

With Pitching Wedge

What to Do

To begin with, there are many types of golf shots which can be made with the pitching wedge. We shall confine this outline of the techniques, however, to the type of short pitch shots most generally used.

1. *The Basic Fairway Pitch Shot:*

    A. Position the ball a few inches to the right of the left heel.
    B. Stand closer to the ball than for normal full iron shots, and use a slightly open stance.
    C. Shorten the grip on the club's handle.
    D. At address, keep the majority of the weight on the left side.
    E. The hands should be *ahead* of the ball at address. Grip the club's handle lightly, but grip *firmly* with the last three fingers of the left hand.
    F. Keep the backswing "short and crisp" with the left arm straight.
    G. Use very little body turn, but almost full shoulder turn. The entire swing is strictly a *hand, arm,* and *wrist* action.
    H. The left knee dips forward, as the right knee braces (but not locks), with *both heels remaining on the ground.*
    I. The wrists cock at approximately hip level.
    J. At the start of the downswing, shift the weight to the left side.
    K. Now pull down with the left arm (which is

kept straight) with the wrists still cocked.
    L. Keep the *head and body still.*
    M. When the hands drop a little below hip level, start uncocking the wrists. The left hip moves out of the way as the arms bring the hands into hitting position.
    N. *Stay down to the shot,* with the hands leading the clubhead *down* and *through* the ball.
    O. At impact, the *back* of the left hand and the *palm* of the right hand face the target.
    P. Keep the *head down, eyes on the ball,* until well *after* impact.
    Q. After impact, the right arm straightens for the full follow-through.
    R. Throw the clubhead out straight toward the target.
    S. Finish the follow-through with the hands fairly high, and the body facing the target. *Don't quit on the shot,* or stub the clubhead into the ground behind the ball.

2. *The Punch Pitch Shot*

    A. Position the ball a little more toward the right foot.
    B. Use the same open stance.
    C. Keep the weight on the *left side* throughout the shot.
    D. Keep the hands *well ahead* of the ball.
    E. Use the same execution for the backswing and downswing, except the backswing is slightly more upright.
    F. Stroke *through* the ball *crisply,* with the hands *low,* and with the left arm *straight* and *firm.*
    G. Keep the follow-through low, and the clubhead *pointing toward the target* at the finish.

3. *The Cut Shot Pitch*

    A. Use the same ball position as for the punch pitch shot.
    B. Use *more* of an open stance, with the weight *kept* on the left side.
    C. Lay the clubface back open, with the hands *slightly behind* the ball.
    D. Take a short upright backstroke, with the wrists breaking sharply.
    E. Use *no body action,* except that the left knee "rolls" to the right on the backswing, and

the right knee to the left on the downswing.

F. On the downswing, cut across the ball from the *outside* of the intended line of flight. Aim slightly to the *left* of the target.

G. Bring the open clubface into and *under* the ball at impact.

H. Swing *through* the ball, again breaking the wrists sharply with the hands finishing higher than for the "punch" pitch.

I. Use this shot *only* if the ball is *sitting up well* in the grass. Don't try this shot off *hard ground* or when the ball is sitting in a divot or a tight lie.

How to Do It

On the backswing, swing the club up with your hands and arms and keep your body coil minimal.

On greenside pitches, set up slightly open with the hands slightly ahead of the ball.

Proper arm and body position as the club enters the impact zone.

Follow-through with the head down and both arms fully extended.

For lofting the ball over a high trap lip, where there is little green surface to land on, use an open stance and clubface. Then stroke firmly, into and under the ball.

Why You Do It

For the basic fairway shot:

ITEM 1A. This is the ball position for most of the shots which are made with every iron club from the No. 2 iron to the wedge, from *level fairway* lies under normal conditions. Most fairway wood shots from similar lies are played from this ball position.

To keep changing the ball position for various clubs of the above range would require you to change the arc of your swing and the manner in which you hit the ball.

Obviously, the ball position must be changed for playing uphill or downhill lies, or when playing shots against a headwind, out of heavy rough, for cut shots, etc.

ITEM 1B. When playing the short pitch shot the stance is quite narrow, since there will be little if any body motion.

Short pitch shots do not require a full swing, so the stance and body alignment will be more open to the target line than for longer iron shots, which automatically shortens the length of the backswing.

When playing this short pitch shot with a pitching wedge, which has a shorter clubshaft than most of the iron clubs, the stance will be much closer to the ball.

For the longer pitch shots, since more body turn will be used for a full swing, the stance will be only slightly open. The swing for such *full* pitch shots is the same as one uses for a No. 8 or No. 9 iron. The loft of the clubface takes care of the distances to be expected for each of these clubs, provided the swing tempo and execution are uniformly the same.

ITEM 1C. For the shorter pitch shots, since the backswing will be less, the hands should be moved down on the grip. This helps promote good club control, and keeps the backswing compact and in one piece.

ITEM 1D. At address, the majority of the weight should be on the *left side.* By keeping body movement to a minimum, and the weight to the left, there is less chance of body sway and a resulting fat hit or skulled shot.

ITEM 1E. Of the greatest importance is the matter of keeping the hands *ahead* of the ball at address. With the hands and weight forward, the player can more easily hit *down* and *through* the ball. In addition, these short pitch shots are not played for *distance* but for *accuracy*. Therefore the club's handle is gripped lightly, with the exception that it should be *firmly* gripped with the *last three fingers* of the left hand. This will prevent the clubface from opening up with the shock of hitting the turf after impact with the ball.

ITEM 1F. Accuracy is aided further by keeping the backstroke short, crisp, and compact. This is quite different from the slower and more complete backswing when the body is being coiled for a *power* hit. One must also remember that the left arm is the "guiding" arm for the swing in *all* golf shots. When it is allowed to collapse, anything can happen—except a good solid hit.

ITEM 1G. In the backstroke, as the club is taken back for a more upright short swing, the shoulders tilt and make *almost* a full turn, but there is little or no turn of the hips. Therefore, the entire swing is mainly performed with the hands, arms, and wrist action.

ITEM 1H. Instead of standing stiff when making the backstroke, the left knee dips forward as the right knee braces, but with *no body sway.* Since there will be a minimum of body movement, *both heels should remain on the ground,* which further prevents body sway.

ITEM 1I. The cocking of the wrists takes place at about hip level, but since the backswing is shorter this is kept at a minimum, where only a one-half or three-quarter backswing is used.

ITEM 1J. Shifting the weight back to the left side at the start of the downswing assures hitting down and through the ball at impact, instead of scooping the shot.

ITEM 1K. The straight left arm is then pulled down, with the wrists still cocked slightly. The right elbow has been brought in close to the right hip. All this helps to control the plane of the downswing, and assures a crisp, solid hit.

ITEM 1L. To allow the head to move on either the backswing or the downswing encourages body sway, resulting in topped or scuffed shots. The head should be considered the axis around which the swing arc is built, even for the short pitch shots.

ITEM 1M. Delaying the uncocking of the wrists until the hands drop below hip level assures a well-controlled, crisp hit at impact.

As the arms bring the hands into a hitting position, the left hip moves out of the way to ensure a smooth downstroke and follow-through.

ITEM 1N. Staying down to the shot, with the hands *leading* the clubhead down and through the ball, assures a solid, crisp impact. When one raises the body at this point only a scooped or topped shot can result.

ITEM 1O. The back of the left hand and the palm of the right hand *must* face the target at impact, and be kept there until the start of the follow-through. To allow the right hand to overtake the left at this point results in a rolling of the wrists to the left, closing the clubface, and causing a pulled shot to the left. The left hand and arm *must stay in control.*

ITEM 1P. Raising the head, and taking the eyes off the ball, just at the point of impact, can only result in a ruined shot, mostly by topping or scuffing. *Keep the head down.* Don't be too anxious to see where the ball is going. If you will only concentrate on what you are doing, and do it well, the ball will usually go where you want it to.

ITEMS 1Q and 1R. The straightening of the right arm, while maintaining control of the left, in the follow-through, throws the clubhead out straight at the target. When this is done, where else can the ball go but straight to your objective?

ITEM 1S. As the body swings around to face the target, the hands raise fairly high in the follow-through. This assures a smooth, full finish, and good balance of the body. Above all, don't quit on the shot, *stubbing the clubhead into the ground* behind the ball. This is the quickest way to top a shot, and lose complete control of the ball's flight in distance and direction.

For the punch pitch shot: The punch pitch shot is the shot to use when you want to hit the ball low, particularly under windy conditions. This type of pitch shot is played differently from a normal pitch.

ITEM 2A. The ball is positioned a little more toward

the right foot, because you want to keep the flight *low.*

ITEM 2B. The stance is open because the backswing is to be *short* and *crisp.*

ITEMS 2C and 2D. It is essential to keep the weight on the left side throughout the entire backswing and downswing, and the hands well ahead of the ball. To overlook these points could cause a badly skulled shot.

ITEM 2E. The backswing is short and crisp, but more upright than for a normal pitch shot, because you are going to punch down on the ball with the hands lower than usual at the point of impact.

ITEM 2F. The downstroke is *crisp,* with the clubhead descending when it meets the ball. The hands are low, and the left arm is kept straight and firm, with firm wrists. This assures hitting into and through the ball sharply.

ITEM 2G. Keep the follow-through *short* and *low,* since the trajectory of the shot will be low, particularly to reduce the effect of headwind or crosswind, when playing this shot under these conditions. With the clubhead pointing to the target at the finish, the ball's flight should also be straight to your objective.

For the cut shot pitch: The cut shot pitch provides a high, "soft" trajectory, with the ball "floating" up to the objective. It is a delicate shot, requiring the *utmost concentration.*

ITEMS 3A, 3B, and 3C. The same ball position is used as for the punch pitch shot, with the stance more open, because the backstroke is shorter, and much more upright, than for a normal pitch shot. The clubface is "laid back" open, with the hands *slightly behind* the ball. This causes the clubhead to cut *into* and *under* the ball from *outside* the line of flight. The weight must be *kept* on the left side.

ITEM 3D. Early in the short upright backswing, the wrists break sharply, to create an upright swing plane, which allows the clubhead to travel into and under the ball as described above.

ITEM 3E. *No body action* is used. "Rolling" the left knee to the right on the backswing, and the right

knee to the left on the downswing, prevents body sway.

ITEMS 3F and 3G. On downswing, by cutting into and under the ball from outside the intended flight line, a clockwise spin is imparted to the ball. Therefore one should aim slightly to the left of the target.

ITEM 3H. Swinging *through* the ball, with the wrists breaking sharply and with the hands finishing high, provides the loft and "floating" action to the ball's trajectory.

ITEM 3I. Since you must be sure to get the clubhead *under* the ball at impact, it must be *sitting up well* in the grass for the cut shot to be successful. If this shot is tried off hard ground, or when the ball is in a tight lie or divot, the sole of the clubhead may bounce into the ball, causing a skulled or topped shot.

The cut shot is not one to be *afraid* of, but one to be *mastered.* Once this has been accomplished, it will get you out of trouble many, many times.

THE LONG AND THE SHORT OF PITCHING

What to Do

Getting your pitching game back in shape at the start of the season is easier than you think, provided you're organized and keep your approach simple. The swing you use for pitches should be the same one you use for full shots, except for minor technical changes in body alignment and ball position.

It helps to divide your pitches into two categories —long and short. Generally, use a pitching wedge for shots from 80 to 100 yards and a sand wedge for shots from 80 yards or less.

On long pitch shots, use a slightly open stance, with the ball a little to the right of center, but keep the shoulders square to the target line. The open stance helps reduce the amount of body turn in the backswing. You swing back to about three-quarter length, a definite aid to control. Standing a little open also helps you to clear your hips to the left on the forward swing, even though the swing is shorter than normal.

On short pitches of around 30 yards, set up with

the shoulders, the hips, and the feet open. Put a little more weight on your left foot. This setup cuts down even more on body action, so essentially your body stays still, and you play the shot mainly with your hands and arms.

After you've practiced these "standard" pitch shots from various distances, you're ready to try several simple variations.

The position of the pin on the green often calls for a higher or lower shot than usual, so the "cut shot pitch," for a soft landing, and the "punch pitch," for run, better be in your repertoire if you expect to play like a pro from relatively close range.

On long pitches, set your feet in an open position, so that if a line were drawn across your toes it would point left of the target.

On short pitches, assume a totally open alignment—setting your feet, knees, hips, and shoulders left of the target.

THE 50-YARD "MONEY" PITCH

What to Do

Medium rough: Play the shot with a sand wedge. The rough will take some backspin off the shot, but the cushion of grass lets you slip the flange of the club under the ball rather than hitting down. What you lose in backspin you'll more than make up for in height.

Play the ball more forward than usual—opposite your left heel. From this lie, you can make contact slightly on the upswing, adding loft to the club. Make a slow swing that's a little fuller than you think is necessary to cover the distance.

Deep rough: Open your stance, open the blade, and play the shot back of center, closer to your right foot. Make a fuller swing to get through the longer grass. The deeper the rough, the harder it is to make the ball travel the distance you want. So if there are any hazards give yourself more leeway to carry them.

THE CHIP SHOT

What to Do

1. Select a club, either a No. 5, 6, or 7 iron, depending upon preference, and the desired roll on the green. By "hooding" the clubface, a pitching wedge is also effective for chip shots to the flagstick.

2. Take an open stance, close to the ball, and choke down on the club's grip.

3. Position the ball in the center of the stance, with the clubhead square to the target, or slightly closed. Keep hands well *ahead* of the clubhead at address.

4. Keep the weight on the left foot. Also keep the head still, and the eyes on the ball.

5. Take the clubhead back *low* to the ground, with the arms and hands, using *no* body action. Use a minimum of wrist break. Keep the right elbow *close* to the body.

6. Don't scoop the shot. The left arm and hand lead the clubhead down and *through* the ball on the downstroke.

7. Make sure the left hand moves past the ball, without the left wrist breaking. The wrists must not "roll" at impact.

8. For a "running" shot, pick a spot on the green for the ball to land (usually about one fourth the distance) on a *level* green, with a roll to the cup for the balance. Adjust this landing spot as necessary for uphill or downhill rolls where the green has such slopes.

9. Strike the ball with a lot of *right* hand, using a putting stroke.

10. For a quick-stopping chip, open the clubface and use a more upright backstroke, taking the clubhead to the outside of the direction line. This creates an outside-in downstroke across the ball for greater backspin.

11. Have the feeling of hitting against a straight left arm, with the follow-through low and smooth.

12. Finish with the clubface, the back of the left hand, and the palm of the right hand square to the target.

If you have just missed the green in the regulation number of strokes (2 or 3 strokes for the par 4 and par 5 holes respectively), this is the little stroke-saver which may put your ball to within easy distance for 1 putt.

How to Do It

The backswing key, on chip shots, is keeping the lower body quiet and swinging the club away low to the ground.

To hit a quick-stopping chip, you must assume an open stance.

The downswing key, on chip shots, is keeping the hands ahead of the ball through impact.

To hit a quick-stopping chip, you must swing outside the direction line (marked by the club on the ground), so that you automatically cut across the ball and impart backspin on it.

Why You Do It

ITEM 1. The chip shot is a lofted putt, and is the type of shot which is generally the most effective when the ball lies just a *short distance* off the green. The loft is often *low,* but must be sufficient to land the ball *on the green* for a run up to the flagstick.

When there is little room between the lie of the ball and the flagstick, use a *pitching wedge* for a short, more lofted chip. (The wedge is also effective for better ball control on *downhill* chips.) Otherwise, use another medium or short iron, depending upon preference.

ITEM 2. The stance will be open, since the backstroke will be short. It will also be quite *close* to the ball, similar to a putting stance, which aids in keeping the clubhead in the proper direction line throughout the entire stroke. Choking down on the grip makes it easier to hit the ball properly, which further increases control.

ITEM 3. The ball is positioned near the center of the stance, because you are going to punch or bump the ball rather than try to scoop it. Generally, the clubface should be square to the target, although a slightly closed clubface may reduce the chance for backspin to occur sufficiently to restrict the ball's run on the green.

Of the greatest importance is the matter of keeping the hands well *ahead* of the clubhead at address, and throughout the entire stroke, which will assure that the ball will be struck *first* sharply, then the turf. When the clubhead passes the hands, scooping the shot generally is the result.

ITEM 4. Keep the weight on the left side throughout the *entire* stroke. Shifting the weight increases the clubhead speed, and affects the precision of the stroke. The head must be kept *still,* and the eyes *fixed* on the ball at all times. This is a delicate precision shot, where absolute control of contact with the ball is necessary for proper direction and distance. Since this is of vital importance, to look up is *fatal.*

ITEM 5. The chip is an exaggerated putt, so the clubhead is taken back *low to the ground.* This shot is performed almost entirely with the arms and hands, and with a minimum of wrist break. Some professionals prefer the "all-wrist" method, with the hands kept over the ball at all times, as a means of controlling the clubface position. We recommend using a minimum of wrist break, however, because for most golfers, to lift the club abruptly on the backswing and snap the wrists on the downstroke often results in scooping the ball up, instead of making a *crisp* stroke *through* the ball, which is much more to be desired. Keeping the right elbow *close to the right hip* provides tight control of the stroke.

ITEM 6. Don't scoop the shot, or try to *lift* the ball up. With the straight left arm and hand *leading* the clubhead *down* and *through* the ball *crisply,* the loft of the clubface will lift the ball sufficiently for your purpose.

ITEM 7. If the left hand moves past the ball without the left wrist breaking, the normal loft of the clubface will provide the proper flight and desired amount of roll for a running chip. When the wrists "roll" at impact, the ball will have a tendency to run sharply after landing on the green. Keep the right hand *under* the left, to keep the clubface *square to the direction line.*

ITEM 8. Only through continual practice can one become reasonably accurate in landing the ball at the proper distance for a safe run to the cup. This landing point must obviously be adjusted for uphill or downhill chip shots, or where the green is either extra hard or soft from excessive watering or rainy weather. It is therefore wise to walk up on the green to the flagstick to check the condition of the surface before making the chip shot. This inspection will help to determine what club to use for either a quick-stopping or running chip.

ITEM 9. Since the chip shot is actually an exaggerated putt, the stroke is similar to a putt, except that it is *more crisp,* with a lot of right-hand action against a *firm* left arm. The clubhead goes sharply *through* the ball, finishing in the follow-through, *pointing straight at the target.*

ITEM 10. For the quick-stopping chip, opening the clubface and taking the clubhead back with an upright backswing, outside the line of flight, is similar to the cut shot pitch, except that the backswing is shorter because less distance is involved. Aim slightly to the *left* of the target for the same reason.

The backspin of the ball coming off the open clubface will impart a left-to-right spin after the landing.

ITEM 11. Unlike the regular cut shot, there is no flipping action of the wrists in the follow-through. The stroke is *crisp* and *low,* with the left arm straight. The farther the right hand is placed *under* the left at impact, the softer the ball will land on the green. For a *quick-stopping* chip, the right hand must *never* roll past the left at impact, or in the follow-through. This would cause the ball to run.

ITEM 12. Once again, for direction accuracy, make sure that during the impact, and in the follow-through, the *clubface,* the *back* of the *left hand,* and the *palm* of the *right hand* are *facing* the target.

CHIPPING FROM BARE LIES

What to Do

When the ball, which has only just missed the green, ends up lying on a very bare piece of ground, use common sense and a simple chipping method. Only a very foolish golfer attempts to use a swing with lots of movement, using the full length of the club, when the chance of a mishit is high.

The experienced player eliminates risk by going down the handle; minimizing wrist movement. He also prefers to play a stroke which is shorter and slower, thus more controlled.

THE STROKE

What to Do

The very basic nature of the stroke enables you to use almost any iron in the bag, depending on the distance to the pin. Even a No. 3 iron could be chosen for a low shot with plenty of forward run.

The hands should be down the grip, so that the right is actually on the shaft.

The slightest wobble in the wrists could cause the ground to be struck first, and the crumbling nature of the sand would definitely cause a fluff. So, with firm wrists, allow the hands to move the clubhead

through the ball, only just scraping the top surface of the soil. There should be no feeling of swinging the club as in conventional shots—more a pushing through of the shaft.

WHEN YOU ARE CHIPPING DOWNHILL

What to Do

When you face a downhill chip and the ball is lying in the manicured fringe with the pin cut 15 to 20 feet from the edge, try playing a pitching wedge.

Stand open to give yourself a better perspective of the hole. This also prevents you from taking the club too far inside the target line on the backswing. To encourage a steep backswing, take a narrow stance, bending more than normal from the waist and placing the majority of your weight on the left side. Choke down on the club for control and swing your hands back to just about knee height, maintaining a stiff left arm. Now cock your right wrist and allow your right elbow to fold naturally into your side.

Start the club down by pulling with your left hand and swing your arms through the shot.

Try to develop an evenly paced rhythm up and back to sink the chip.

THE SAND TRAP SHOT

What to Do

1. For normal trap shots, determine:

   A. The distance to the flagstick.
   B. How high is the lip of the trap in front of the ball?
   C. Is the sand wet or dry?
   D. Is the ball sitting up well, or buried?

2. If the sand is dry, and the ball is sitting up well, anchor the feet *firmly* and stand well over the ball. Keep the weight on the left side.

3. Grip the club's handle low, and play the ball off the *left heel,* with an open stance. *Do not*

ground your clubhead. It is against the rules of the United States Golf Association.

4. Open the clubface and take an exceedingly upright backswing, usually a three-quarter swing. Aim slightly to the *left* of the target. Take the clubhead back *outside* the flight line.

5. Keep the left arm straight, and cock the wrists sharply.

6. Keep the right elbow close to the body on the backswing.

7. On the downswing, cut across the ball from the outside in.

8. Hit the *sand* approximately 1 to 2 inches *behind* the ball, depending upon the texture of the sand, and the distance required for the shot. Keep the eyes *fixed on this spot in the sand,* not on the *ball.*

9. *Don't stub the clubhead into the sand.* Follow through *completely.* Adjust the swing and the force of the stroke, with the distances required.

10. For a buried lie, close or hood the clubface at address by moving the hands ahead of the clubhead and playing the ball back toward the right foot a little. Swing harder than normal. *Open* the clubface where a *quick stop* is desired. Break the wrists sharply in the backswing, and stroke firmly with *lots of right hand,* entering the sand as close as possible behind the ball, with a slicing action.

11. On all sand trap shots, *stay down to the ball.*

12. Where the front lip of the trap is low, and the ball is *sitting up well,* on *wet sand,* a chip shot may be employed, or even a putter, but *hit the ball cleanly and firmly, not the sand behind it.* Play the ball to the right of the center of the stance for these shots.

How to Do It

When the ball is sitting up in the sand, increase your recovery power by setting your body and the clubface "open."

Keeping your head perfectly still, swing the club on an upright backswing angle.

To extract the ball from a buried lie, you must play it back in your stance. Also, hood the blade of the club by setting your hands in a forward position.

On the downswing, hit the sand 1 to 2 inches behind the ball and follow through completely.

The buried ball, or "fried-egg" lie.

To set yourself up for a sharp, downward blow directly behind the ball, you must employ an extremely upright backswing.

Why You Do It

ITEMS 1A, 1B, 1C, and 1D. When your ball lands in a greenside sand trap, the first thing you should do before attempting to make your shot is to size up the situation carefully. Don't just grab a club out of your bag, rush over to your ball, and whale away at it.

Take time to determine the best way to get out, and as close as possible to the flagstick. There is really *no reason to fear* a sand trap shot. All it takes is a little know-how, and confidence. Even the pros get into these hazards occasionally, but they *know* how to get out of them, and *so can you.*

First, study and absorb the points covered earlier, on "What to Do." Then select the club to properly execute the shot in the manner described, and make your shot. If you study the techniques outlined, and *practice* religiously, it won't be long before you will become a fine trap player.

ITEM 2. If the sand is *dry,* and the ball is sitting up well, anchor the feet *firmly* by twisting them around in the sand until they are below the loose sand on top and feel as though they are on solid footing. This is to prevent the feet from slipping, with possible loss of balance and body sway, while executing the shot.

Stand well over the ball, with the weight *kept on the left side* throughout the swing. This is due to the fact that the backswing will be short and very upright and, with the weight to the left, the clubhead will cut across and *through the sand,* in *back* of the ball, in a firm but smooth stroke, instead of "scooping" the ball up.

ITEM 3. The club's handle should be gripped low for control. In addition, digging the feet into the sand will make them a few inches *lower* than for a normal fairway shot on level ground so that the ball will be that much higher than the feet, and closer to the hands. This requires a sharp and short swing plane.

At address, the clubhead should be held behind the ball, and slightly above the sand to prevent grounding it, which is against the rules.

The stance is open, which makes it easier to control the shot, taking the clubhead back *outside* the flight line on the backswing, and cutting across to the *inside* on the downswing. Applying this cut into the *sand behind the ball* prevents slicing into the

sand too deeply, or stubbing the clubhead into the sand and stopping it there. The open stance also allows the left hip to move out of the way on the downswing, assuring a *full follow-through.*

Playing the ball forward off the left heel, or even off the left instep or toe, compensates for the inch or more behind the ball the clubhead will enter the sand, as opposed to a normal fairway iron shot, where the ball is positioned slightly to the right of the left heel. This enables the impact to be made at, or slightly before, the bottom of the swing arc.

ITEM 4. The open clubface enables the player to slice through the sand in back of the ball, and *under* it, instead of digging the clubhead into the sand. It also provides the desired loft to the shot for clearing the lip of the trap, and for settling quickly on the green.

The explosion shot should be a smooth, easy stroke, never made with full force. Therefore, the backswing is short, and sharply upright. The open stance assures taking the clubhead back *outside* the flight line. Because the downstroke will also be from the outside in, and the stance and clubface are open, a left-to-right spin will be imparted to the ball. Therefore, one should aim slightly to the *left* of the target.

ITEM 5. With the open stance, the position of the right hip at address helps to control the hands from coming back in too flat a swing arc, and aids in a quick cocking of the wrists. The left arm, however, must be kept straight.

ITEM 6. Keeping the right elbow close to the body assures breaking the wrists early in the backswing, making it sharply upright.

ITEM 7. Since one must slice the sand *in back of* and *under* the ball on the downswing, this stroke must be made from *outside* the flight line. The *left hand and arm* lead the clubhead down and *through* the sand, smoothly but *firmly.*

ITEM 8. It is the *sand* that lifts the ball as the clubhead cuts under the ball 1 to 2 inches in back, depending upon the flight distance required. The clubhead makes *no contact with the ball itself.* To do so would result in picking it off too cleanly, probably sending it completely over the green to the other side. So the eyes must be fixed on the proper spot in the sand to hit into.

ITEM 9. Only a miracle will get the ball out of the trap when the clubhead is stubbed into the sand and stopped there. *Follow through completely,* finishing with the clubhead fairly high. Only through *practice* will one be able to judge the amount of backswing and the force of the swing necessary for various distances required. Such practice is *well worth the effort.*

ITEM 10. For a partly buried lie, the clubface is closed or "hooded" at address with the hands *ahead* of the clubhead. This reduces the chance that the rounded sole of the sand wedge will skim across the top of the sand and skull the shot. Instead the clubhead will cut deeper into the sand under the ball, and this requires a little more force in the swing. Also, playing the ball back toward the right foot a little assures hitting *through* the sand with a *downward* blow. In contrast, in a buried lie, where the flagstick is close to the near edge of the green, and a quick stop is desired, the clubface must be *open.* Breaking the wrists early makes the backswing sharply upright. This creates a sharply vertical downswing, with the *right hand* driving the clubhead down into the sand behind the ball in a slicing action. Hitting the sand as close as possible to the ball will "pop" the ball out with more backspin than with the normal trap shot.

ITEM 11. On all trap shots, it is essential to *stay down to the ball* instead of lifting the head, or trying to scoop the ball up by raising the body. *Flex the knees, and keep the head still.*

ITEM 12. On wet, compacted sand, with the ball sitting up well, and the front lip of the trap *low,* one may either use a sand wedge or chip out. Either shot can be carried off successfully if executed properly. If a wedge is chosen, the clubface is opened wide, and the club taken back *low* to the *outside* of the direction line. On the downswing, the clubhead enters the sand about an inch behind the ball, cutting under it *slightly* but not digging into the sand. The downstroke is naturally made from the outside in. Above all, make sure that the clubhead cuts *through* the sand behind the ball, and does not strike the ball first or a skulled shot will result.

If a chip shot is preferred *use a No. 8 iron, not a sand wedge.* Be sure to hit the ball *first* cleanly in the same manner as when playing a chip shot off the grass. *Never* try a chip shot out of *dry, light sand.*

If the trap is fairly flat, and the front lip also low and flat, a putter may be used with good success. The ball is positioned similar to a regular putt on the green. Strike the ball cleanly, however, and with the *toe* of the clubhead. This will tend to reduce the backspin of the ball and provide a better roll.

CLIMBING OVER A HIGH BUNKER WALL IS SIMPLE

What to Do

To loft the ball over a high lip of a bunker, putting "stop" on it, try employing a "scooping" action. Basically, this technique requires a dipping action both on the backswing and downswing, which in turn allows you to spoon the ball out.

Address the ball with an open stance. This allows your arms to swing freely back and through, on a steep plane. Open the clubface slightly and play the ball off your left heel with the majority of your weight forward.

To help you get the ball up, grip the club with your right hand firmly turned under and drop your right shoulder slightly. The stronger grip helps keep the clubface open and induces the scooping action.

To achieve this scooping effect, leave more weight on your left side while you swing up, and then, more weight on your right side as you swing the club down and through the ball. The higher you want to hit the shot, the more weight you move back to your right side at impact.

TIPS ON PUTTING

What to Do

1. First, examine the grass, and the slope of the green, in the direct line of your putt as follows:

   A. For foreign matter such as leaves, twigs, etc.

B. For repairable depressions or divots. Use a wooden tee for repairs.

C. Which way is the grass grain growing—toward your line of putt or with it?

D. Is the putt uphill or downhill? How much?

E. Is there a lateral slope to the right, or the left?

F. Is the grass on the green closely mowed, or a little high?

G. Is the green hard or soft? Wet or dry?

H. If "casual water" is in line with your putt, or where your ball rests, it is permissible, according to The Rules of Golf, to move the ball without penalty, to a point no nearer the cup that has no water in your line.

2. Sight the line of the putt from in back of the ball.

3. Pick out a spot on the green to which you will aim your putt.

4. Take the stance *with the weight on the left side, and with the toes of both feet even* on the line parallel to where you want the ball to travel.

5. Stand close enough to the ball so that the putter blade is *flat* on the ground, and with your eyes right over the ball. Keep the hands *close* to the body.

6. Grip the club comfortably, either at top of the handle or down a couple of inches.

7. Grip club's handle with both hands close together, using a reverse overlap (the left forefinger extended down, and outside the last two or three fingers of the right hand). The back of the left hand and the palm of the right hand should face the target, with both hands slightly *under* the club's handle.

8. *Remove all thoughts* from your mind except making the proper putting stroke. *Relax.*

9. Position the ball about 1 or 2 inches to the right of the left toe.

10. Keep the *head still, and the body motionless.*

11. Keep the putterblade *low to the ground* on the backswing. Gauge the backswing distance by the length of the putt. The longer the putt, the longer the backstroke. Stroke all putts with about the same force, except the exceptionally long ones. It is the distance of the backstroke that controls the length of the ball's roll. Let the clubhead do the work.

12. Keep the clubhead square to the line of the putt, particularly on the forward stroke. The arms do most of the work, with the left forearm sliding gently forward in a *straight* path after the ball is hit. Follow through about 5 inches past the original ball position. The clubhead *must* be *accelerating* at impact. Don't quit on the stroke.

13. Push the putterblade well through the ball, and toward the hole as indicated above.

14. If the slope of the green, or "break," is to the right, aim slightly to the left of the cup, increasing the aim in this manner if the break is sharp. If it is to the left, aim to the right in the same way.

15. Don't jab the putt, but stroke *firmly,* particularly on *short putts.* Don't "baby" the putt.

SOME THINGS TO CONSIDER

The regulation cup is 4.25 inches wide. An American ball is 1.68 inches wide.

If the ball stops even with the cup, and more than one half the ball is over the edge, the ball will usually drop in.

One half the ball's diameter is .84 inches. If just a little more than one half the ball stops at the side lip of the cup, and hangs over the side, the actual width of the target for a possible drop is not 4.25 inches, but closer to 5.75 inches. This increases the margin for error and creates a bigger target.

How to Do It

Putting Address: Position the ball to the right of the left foot. Grip the handle at the top, with the hands close together. Stand close to the ball so that the putterblade is flat on the ground, and the eyes are over ball. The back of the left hand and the palm of the right hand should face the target.

Putting Backstroke: Take the putterblade back low to the ground, and square to the target (or line of putt). Increase or decrease the backstroke to fit the distance of the putt. Keep the body and head motionless.

To groove a good backstroke, putt between two clubs.

Putting Downstroke: The ball remains in the picture to show the approximate distance of the clubhead follow-through, past the original ball position after impact. Keep the clubhead square to the line of the target. The arms do most of the work, but the left forearm slides gently forward after the ball is stroked.

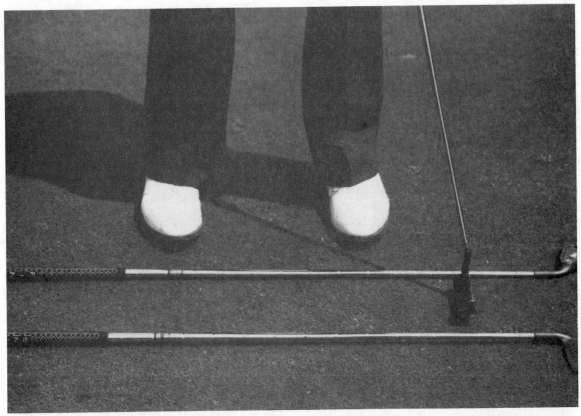

To groove a good downstroke, putt between two clubs.

To groove an accelerating downstroke, in practice, first set a coin a few inches in front of the ball.

Second, try and brush the putterblade over the coin as you swing through toward the hole.

Why You Do It

In the preceding pages, the tips outlining what to do in putting are for the most part self-explanatory. Therefore, instead of a cross-reference to each item, as in the case of other subjects, only general comments follow.

Anyone who has played the game of golf for any length of time knows how important good putting is to good scoring. This phase of the game accounts for one half or more of *all* the strokes which are made in a round of golf.

Unless one learns to be a good putter, he will never score well. If he does learn to putt well, or better than average, he will win many a match game with his friends, even though a few other shots from the tee or fairway are not executed well.

The regulation number of putting strokes for an 18-hole round is 36, or 2 for each hole. When this average can be reduced by several 1-putt greens, it is not hard to understand the effect this can have on the scoring result.

With consistent practice, and adherence to the basic techniques which we have tried to outline, *anyone* can become a good putter.

GENERAL COMMENTS ON WHY YOU DO IT

It is important to check the direction in which the grass grain grows before you start to make your putt—the ball will usually roll in the direction of the grain near the end of its roll.

At this same point in the roll, it will break with the lateral slope of the green's surface.

If the grain is *toward* you in your putting line, you must stroke more firmly. The same thing applies to *uphill* putts.

If the grass is growing *away* from you in your line, stroke a little easier, with a shorter backstroke.

The grain of the grass will appear *lighter* in color when it grows *away* from you, and *darker* when it grows *toward* you.

If the green surface is *hard,* or the grass surface closely mowed, the ball will roll easier and faster. When the grass is longer, or the surface soft or dewy, there is more resistance to the ball's roll.

Picking a spot along the line of the putt to aim at helps one to keep the putt on line, and improves concentration. It provides an objective other than the cup itself. This is important when the spot chosen is 5 or 6 inches in front of the cup, but to either side, when you are expecting a break to left or right. Without this objective, one is simply *guessing.*

When the toes of both feet are directly parallel to the putting line, there is less chance for a push to the right, or a pulled shot to the left.

Keeping most of the weight on the left side, and back on the heels, helps keep the *body still.* Since the stroke will be to the left, there should be less chance of *moving the body with the stroke.* Some professionals advocate having the weight *even* on both feet, and some seem to have more of it on the right side. The main thing is to be *comfortable* and *relaxed,* with the head and body kept *perfectly still* during the entire stroke.

While for normal *level* ground putts the ball position at address should be slightly to the right of the left toe, this position varies for *uphill* or *downhill* putts. For *uphill* putts, play the ball more in line with the *toe* of the left foot. For *downhill* putts, play it *farther back to the right,* toward the right foot.

One should stand over the ball quite close, with the head bent down, and the eyes on the ball. Also, keep the hands *close to the body* for better control of the stroke. If one reaches out for the ball at address, it is difficult to keep the putterblade *square* to the line, in either the back or forward stroke. This could cause either a pushed or a pulled shot. Keeping the back of the left hand and the palm of the right hand facing the target helps to keep the putting stroke square to the line also. When the left hand is slightly *under* the shaft's handle, it is an aid to prevent *pulling* the putt to the left. The right hand should be slightly under, and well *behind,* the shaft's handle for a more positive stroke forward, *square* to the line.

The "reverse overlap" grip is used by most professionals: the left forefinger is extended down and over the little finger or the last two fingers of the right hand. This helps to control the hands and again keeps the stroke on line. Putting is strictly a *right-hand* push with a left-hand guide.

The distance of the backstroke generally controls and determines the distance of the roll of the ball, since the forward force of the stroke is approximately the same for most putts. For longer putts, a slightly firmer impact with the ball is generally necessary. Keep the putterblade *low to the ground in the backstroke.*

One must always be sure that the putterblade is *accelerating* at impact and a follow-through is employed. This helps to assure a firm impact, and keeps the ball on line. To *quit* on the stroke at impact ruins the straightness of the ball's roll, and also generally leaves the ball far short of the cup.

If a forward press is employed, this is done *only with the hands, not the body, as for example, in the case of a forward press used in a tee shot.* The putting forward press helps to produce a rhythmic start of the backstroke.

Some golfers employ the "pendulum" swing, and are known as "strokers." Others use a shorter backstroke, and strike the ball more firmly. They are called "jabbers." The first use both arms and wrists, and the second, mostly the wrists. In either type of stroke the impact is not "jerky," but *smooth* and *firm.* Practice both ways and decide for yourself which type of stroke is best suited for *your* style.

When practicing, try to sink all the putts you can from approximately *5 feet,* until you feel that you can sink *all* or *most* putts from this distance. Then move back a little, and improve your accuracy for greater distances. If you always attempt to get close enough in the first putt for an *easy* second, *some* of the first putts are bound to drop.

A main point is to keep the mind *free of doubts* or other distracting thoughts when making your putting stroke. *Think positively,* and *relax.*

WHEN TO ALTER YOUR PUTTING SETUP

To putt consistently well, you need to groove a sound technique. There are times, however, when a change in your putting stroke is beneficial—on slow greens, on long putts, in a strong wind, and on downhill putts.

SLOW GREEN

What to Do

On a slow green, play the ball farther forward than its normal position off the left heel. This helps catch it more on the upswing, which lessens the

The normal ball position for putting.

backspin imparted to the ball. Thus, the ball rolls more smoothly.

Although playing the ball farther back on fast greens would seem to make sense, we don't recommend it, primarily because it will distort how you perceive your alignment, and you'll tend to push your putts.

Simply play the ball a little farther up, about one ball width, on slow greens. Then go back to your normal position when you return to average greens.

LONG PUTTS

What to Do

Long putts, of say, over 30 feet, are a problem for many golfers. More often than not, golfers either roll these up to 15 feet long, or the same distance short. If this is happening to you, then probably the fault originates in your posture—you crouch as much on your long putts as on your short putts.

The deeper you crouch for long putts, the more you need a very wristy, almost violent action to get the ball to the hole, exactly the opposite of what you want on the putting green. First, the smoother the stroke, the better. Second, a stiff-wristed stroke is always superior to a wristy one. There is a simple way to avoid the wristy pitfall on long putts—simply stand more erect instead of crouching. This posture will help you produce more leverage and a more forceful stroke, with no extra effort, which can throw you off balance on a putt just as quickly as on a full swing. By standing more upright you can easily make a long, fluid stroke, one that you can control.

Standing more erect also helps you determine the line of the putt. Most important, it helps you judge distance, the essential on long putts. Most 3-putt greens don't occur because a putt is off line—usually your worst effort won't be more than 4 or 5 feet on either side of the hole. Getting the right distance is the problem, and standing more upright will help you overcome it. Your lag putts will definitely improve with this technique.

The best ball position for putting on slow greens.

The "wrong" posture for long putts.   The "right" posture for long putts.

IN A STRONG WIND

What to Do

When it's very gusty, golfers often putt badly because the wind makes them sway just as it makes the flagstick bend. The result is almost always an off-center hit and a poor putt, so crouch to anchor yourself firmly at address. Crouching will lower your center of gravity, thus you'll be in a solid position to stroke the ball squarely.

In extremely high winds, you may also go to a wider stance than usual. Don't overdo this; a couple of inches is enough. Too wide a stance will upset your normal stroke. If you have a putter with a longer shaft than normal, you might also choke down about an inch. However, crouching will usually be enough to keep you steady.

There is the dilemma of having to sink a very long putt in a strong wind. In that case, it's probably best to ignore my advice about long putts and still crouch, so that you ensure flush contact with the ball, but take a little extra time to get the feel of how hard to hit the ball.

DOWNHILL PUTTS

What to Do

A steeply downhill putt presents a special problem: that of controlling the speed of the putt. It takes only a small flaw in your judgment or stroke for the ball to finish very short or very long, which sets you up for a 3-putt green. To help you stroke these putts the proper distance, try addressing the ball slightly toward the toe of the putter. This produces a sort of "dead" hit; you can stroke the ball more firmly off the toe and it won't roll as far as if you had hit it on the sweet spot.

It may seem that hitting the ball off the toe would open the blade at impact unless you gripped the putter more firmly, but that's not true. You can use your normal grip pressure, provided you keep the putterhead going through the ball. Many golfers stop the forward motion of the blade too soon after impact, because they're afraid to go ahead and stroke the ball on downhill putts. That's what

On windy days, employ this wider putting stance.

On downhill putts, address the ball off the toe end of the putterblade.

A close-up view of the proper putterface-to-ball position for handling downhill putts.

causes those off-line putts. This toe hit will allow you to make a bold stroke without the danger of the ball rolling off the green.

PUTTING ERRORS

Do's and Don'ts

People use several different putting styles and strokes. Choose one which gets the best results for *you*.

Here are three common errors (E) and their corrections (C).

1. (E) Ball stops *short* of the hole.
   (C) Don't "baby" the stroke. Stroke firmly, particularly on uphill putts. Check for grass grain growing *against* the line of the putt.

2. (E) The ball runs *past* the hole.
   (C) Pick a spot on the green approximately 6 inches in front of the hole to aim your putt. Gauge your putt to reach this spot, and to roll into the cup from that point. Where there is a slope to the green (left to right or right to left), estimate the amount of the break and choose a similar spot slightly in front of the hole, but to either side, to which you will aim your putt.

3. (E) Pushed or pulled shots.
   (C) Keep the stroke *square* to the line at *impact*, and follow through at least 5 inches past the original ball position at address.

5

Professional Tips

In the preceding chapters we have attempted to provide the basic techniques; these are not hard to learn, provided you first seek professional instruction, and then are willing to study and practice what has been taught. There is no other way.

Now we come to corrections for various stroking errors (faults experienced by all golfers, even the best, from time to time). Also in this chapter, we'll show you how to deal with abnormal conditions, abnormal lies, and teach you how to tackle trouble spots. You'll even learn the art of working the ball around, over, and under obstacles, so that you're fully prepared for any on-course situation.

Neither the beginner or the more experienced player ever attains perfection in all the shots he is called upon to make. Therefore, the game is always a challenge.

This is the main reason most people love the game of golf once they have tried it. The longer they play, the more this feeling grows. There is just no game like it, bar none.

Many players have the idea that they are playing some other person as their opponent. To the degree that they want to achieve a lower score, they are. If one is careful to make as few mistakes as possible, and his playing companion does not use the same care, however, sooner or later the one with less mistakes will come out ahead.

So play your *real* opponent, *the golf course.* And, in addition to learning how to correct a swing fault in the middle of a round, learn the shots which will help you to beat the course.

CORRECTIONS

For Skulling

1. Stand closer to the ball.

2. Keep the *head still* throughout the swing. Keep your *eyes on the ball.*

3. Concentrate on swinging smoothly, not on looking up to see where the ball goes.

4. Don't stiffen or lock the right knee on the backswing.

5. Make sure the weight is shifted to the right leg during the backswing, but be sure to *shift the full weight to the left foot on the downswing.*

6. Don't try to lift the ball into the air with body action, or a flick of the wrists.

For Scuffing

1. Don't try to "kill" the ball. Swing smoothly.

2. Don't bend the left knee too much on the backswing.

3. Keep the arms *fully extended* at the start of the backswing.

4. Don't allow the right side of the body to sag.

5. *Shift the weight completely to the left on the downswing.*

Fat hits are mainly caused by failing to shift the weight to the left foot on the downswing.

For Skying

1. Tee the ball no further forward than the *left instep* for driving off the tee, so that impact is made just after the *bottom* of the *swing arc has been reached,* and at the *start* of the upswing.

2. Don't lift the clubhead sharply on the backswing. Keep it *low to the ground* for the first 12 to 24 inches.

3. Don't chop down at the ball.

4. Don't roll the wrists drastically.

For Slicing

1. Grip the club so that at least two or three knuckles of the left hand are showing.

2. Use a square or slightly closed stance.

3. Start the backswing *low* and *slow.* Keep the right elbow close to the body until the top of the backswing.

4. Do not break the wrists until the hands reach hip height.

5. Keep a *firm* grip on the club's handle.

6. On the downswing, don't *reach* for the ball, but swing from inside out.

For Hooking

1. Grip the club with both hands placed more to the *left* than customarily. Only one or two knuckles of the left hand should show.

2. Start the backswing with the left hand in control, and maintain this control throughout the entire swing.

3. Do not roll the wrists too actively.

4. At the top of the backswing, make sure that the right wrist is *under* the club's handle.

5. On the downswing, don't let the right hand dominate.

For Shanking

1. Stand farther from the ball at address.

2. Keep the weight even, on both soles and *heels* of the feet. Don't lurch forward.

3. Keep the right elbow close to the body on the downswing.

4. Don't *reach* for the ball, or swing across it from outside in.

5. Keep the right shoulder *behind* the ball.

WINDY DAY PLAY

What to Do

If you want to be a complete golfer, you will have to be able to beat the wind.

The most difficult winds are from left to right and right to left, but if you master the "knockdown draw" and the "knockdown fade" you can hit the ball close to the flag.

The idea is to hit the punch draw into a left-to-right crosswind and the fade into a wind blowing from the other direction. Both shots will hold their line and travel the proper distance because they fly underneath the wind and drop swiftly on the putting surface—a big plus on fast running greens.

"THE KNOCKDOWN DRAW"

How to Hit It

Simply play the ball about 2 inches farther back in your stance than normal. Use two more clubs than usual for the distance at hand. In other words if the shot normally calls for a No. 9 iron, take a 7. Choke down on the grip, about two inches, as this adjustment enhances your control of the shot.

When you address the ball, make sure the clubface is square to the target. You also want to use a square stance. An open stance would cause you to clear your hips too quickly on the downswing, pulling the club across the line with the result being a block to the right.

Simply take a three-quarter swing with little wrist cock, and swing the club down with your arms. But, most importantly, allow your right forearm to turn over through impact to encourage the clubface to close slightly, a move that will allow you to produce the draw spin.

THE "KNOCKDOWN FADE"

How to Hit It

Again take two clubs more than usual, choke down on the grip, and play the ball back in the stance. However, stand closer to the ball. This will help you make a more upright backswing and hit down more sharply on the ball, both of which are necessary for producing a low flying fade. You also want a slightly open stance, to encourage you to lift the club up outside the line on the backswing and to pull across the line coming through. You should swing back only to a three-quarter position with little wrist cock. From there, swing down across the target line, while preventing the right forearm from turning over drastically and the wrists from releasing fully.

RAINY DAY PLAY

What to Do

1. Keep the club grips dry. Wipe each handle and clubhead with a towel after each shot.

2. Use *one* club *more* than usual for all *full* shots. In wet weather the air is heavier, which reduces the distance of the ball's flight.

3. Hit the ball *cleanly.* Try to "sweep" the ball off the ground wherever possible. The clubhead has a tendency to dig too deep into soggy ground. Also, wet grass between the clubface and the ball could spoil the shot.

4. Lift the ball away from "casual water." This is okay under U.S.G.A. rules.

5. For pitch shots, aim as close to the target as possible. Wet greens or casual water restrict the ball's run up to the cup.

6. Use a chip shot or putt the ball out of sand traps wherever possible. A sand wedge will usually bounce off wet sand unless played perfectly.

7. When just off the edge of the green don't try to chip, or run the ball up to the target. (Pitch it.) Casual water or heavy, wet greens slow down the roll of the ball.

8. Play the ball off the left toe, and stroke a putt more firmly than usual, particularly on uphill putts.

9. See your pro shop for rain gloves, clothes, umbrellas, and towels. These articles can be carried in your golf bag, and are lifesavers when you are caught in a sudden rainstorm.

10. In wet weather, don't leave your golf clubs in the trunk of your automobile. Excessive moisture can cause your wood clubs to swell.

ABNORMAL LIES

Sidehill Lie (ball above feet)

1. Shorten the grip on the club's handle.

2. Play the ball to the right of the target, or open the stance.

3. Play the ball slightly more off the right foot.

4. Swing easier, with a shorter backswing than usual.

5. Swing smoothly in the hitting zone. Don't fall away from the shot.

Sidehill Lie (ball below feet)

1. Stand closer to the ball.

2. Use a slightly closed stance, or play the ball to the left of the target.

3. Play the ball in the center of the stance, with the hands slightly ahead of the ball.

4. Keep the weight on the heels with the knees flexed. Stay down to the ball, but don't reach for it.

Severe Uphill Lie

1. Use a straighter-faced club than usual, to prevent excess loft in the shot.

2. Take a practice swing to determine the place where the clubhead touches the ground.

3. Play the ball off the "high" foot.

4. Aim to the right of the target.

5. Keep the weight even on both feet.

6. Swing along the slope of the hill.

Severe Downhill Lie

1. Use a more lofted club to get the ball in the air more quickly.

2. Take a practice swing to determine the place where the clubhead touches the ground.

3. Play the ball off the "high" foot.

4. Aim to the left of the target.

5. Keep the weight even on both feet.

6. Use a more upright backswing.

7. On the downswing, follow the slope of the ground.

TACKLING TROUBLE SPOTS

From Fairway Trap

1. Play the shot the same way as for any other fairway shot, provided the lip of the trap is low enough to clear.

2. Hit the ball cleanly, using either a wood club or an iron, depending upon the distance to the target.

From Fairway Divot Hole

1. Play the ball closer to the right foot.

2. Close the clubface slightly.

3. Hit down on the ball, using plenty of wrist action.

4. Use a more lofted wood club for longer shots.

From Deep Rough

1. Use a well-lofted club (one that will get you out in 1 shot). You may have to sacrifice some distance, depending upon the lie of the ball.

2. Open the clubface wide. Long grass tends to close the clubface in. Play the ball more toward the right foot.

From Water

1. If at least half of the ball is above water, you can recover by playing a lofted iron.

2. Employ a smooth three-quarter backswing.

3. Hit down sharply, driving the clubhead into the water, immediately in back of the ball.

4. Keep the weight on the left foot throughout the swing and follow-through.

From Grassy Banks

1. Take an open stance.

2. Play the ball off the "high" foot.

3. Open the clubface.

4. Swing harder than normal to compensate for the higher trajectory expected.

5. Hit the ball before the turf.

MAKE THE BALL "TALK"

How to Hit Around, Over, and Under Obstacles

If you think that only the pros can deliberately shape shots and hit the ball high and low, you're wrong. Putting these shots in your repertoire is easy. Besides improving your scoring, learning to work the ball helps you develop a better swing.

HITTING THE CONTROLLED HOOK

What to Do

To make the ball curve left, align your feet and shoulders to the right of the target but close the clubface—by aiming the leading edge of the club at the target—before you take your grip. Swing up and down along the path set up by your shoulders so that the ball starts to the right; the closed blade puts right-to-left spin on the ball, hooking it back to the target.

Paramount to producing a controlled hook is the proper setup: aim right of your final target.

Adjust for the controlled slice by setting up left of your final target.

HITTING THE CONTROLLED SLICE

What to Do

To make the ball curve right, reverse the procedure for the hook. Set up with your feet and shoulders aligned to the left of the target, but open the clubface by aiming the leading edge at the target. Then take your grip. Again your swing path is governed by shoulder alignment, so you swing through to the left of the target, and the ball starts in that direction. Because the clubface is open, the slice-spin brings the ball back to the target.

HITTING THE HIGH BALL

What to Do

To get a higher-than-normal trajectory, play the ball a little more forward in your stance, increasing the effective loft of the club. Move your right foot a little more to the right so you set more weight on it. Swing back normally, but on the downswing keep the weight on the right foot longer than usual, which encourages you to swing up on the ball.

HITTING THE LOW BALL

What to Do

To deloft the club, play the ball back in your stance. Spread your left foot a little more to the left and put more weight there. During the swing, keep the weight on the left foot longer than usual to drive the ball down.

6

Golf Equipment

What kind of equipment should one acquire when starting to learn this wonderful game of golf?

Certain items are absolutely necessary. Others can be acquired later, as a means of further enhancing the pleasure of playing the game, in addition to helping promote more efficiency in the execution of easy or difficult golf shots.

Collectively, all of these items represent a substantial investment. When this is balanced against the many years of healthful pleasure one receives from their use, however, the dividends far outweigh the investment.

THE MOST IMPORTANT ITEMS, INCLUDING
AVERAGE PRICES*

Full set of new and completely balanced golf clubs	$750
Starter set, (Nos. 1 and 3 woods, Nos. 3, 5, 7, and 9 irons, and putter)	$150
Used clubs (complete set)	$125
Golf bag	$100
Golf pull cart	$ 75
Golf glove	$ 12
Golf shoes (1 pair)	$ 75
Head covers (set of 4)	$ 30
Golf balls (per dozen)	$ 26
Golf umbrella	$ 25
Golf apparel–rain gear	$140

* All prices shown are subject to change, depending upon the current market.

GOLF EQUIPMENT

What to Buy?

In golf, of necessity, one of the first things that must be considered by the beginner of *any* age is just what equipment is needed to get a good start at learning the game.

Naturally, the game cannot be played at all without a few golf clubs and a ball. In addition to these, one would of course want to think about having a good pair of golf shoes, to help provide a firm footing while executing the golf shots that will be required on various ground surfaces. And other items, such as a bag for the golf clubs, possibly a golf cart to carry them, a golf glove to help in gripping the clubs firmly, and such items of golf apparel as are necessary to help one feel comfortably dressed, and which will permit perfect freedom of movement when swinging the clubs.

But to get back to the matter of golf clubs. What kind should one buy, and how many?

Frankly, the answer depends largely on two major points: how much can you afford to invest, and what does your PGA teaching professional think you should have?

Assuming for the moment that the investment in proper equipment will not be an insurmountable problem, let us look at the second point—the teacher's recommendation:

First, we must assume that you have decided to

The typical pro shop.

take lessons from a competent instructor. As we have repeatedly stated, this book will *help* you learn the game. You will still require the services of a good instructor, however, to teach the physical execution of all golf shots.

Second, because of your ability to learn rapidly and make excellent progress, your instructor may see a good future for you in the game. If so, he may recommend that you be properly fitted with a full complement of golf clubs right at the start.

There is no denying that a complete new set of clubs would give any new player a feeling of pride of ownership. By having a full set of all of the required clubs, moreover, the student will be able to learn the distances he can achieve with each club during his session on the practice range. This becomes mighty important to learn, since it will help him to know what particular club to use for various distances while playing a regular practice round on the golf course, and later on in tournament competition.

PRO-FITTED GOLF CLUBS

What kind of golf clubs are you now using?

Are they fitted to your personal requirements?

Is your set of clubs complete for all golf shots you may be required to make?

There are several important factors in the selection of golf clubs for each player. Among them are:

Your athletic makeup.
Your physical specifications and aptitudes.
Your temperament.
Your age.
Club quality, length, and weight, shaft flexibility, etc.

These are factors your experienced PGA professional considers in prescribing clubs for *your individual needs.*

For example, depending on the length of his arms, most of the time a taller player needs a longer

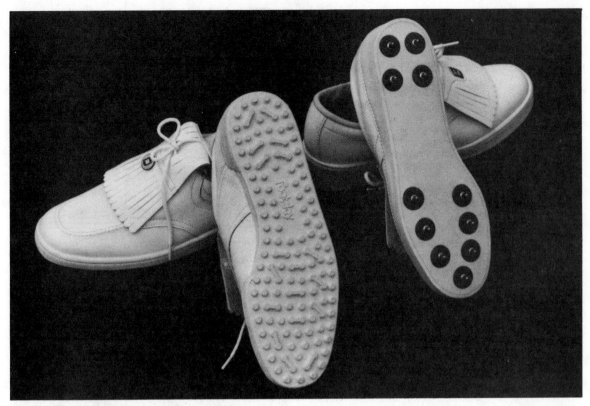

Modern-day spikeless and spiked golf shoes.

shaft than a person shorter in height.

An older person needs a whippy, flexible shaft to help him gain clubhead speed for added distance. Also, the swing weight should be carefully chosen for a player's *individual swing.*

Many golfers, particularly those playing less frequently, are using clubs with *none* of the above individual factors having been considered. Some do not even have a full complement of clubs. This might be all right for a beginner who buys only a starter set for economy's sake, but sooner or later a *completely balanced* set, fitted to *your* individual requirements, cannot help but improve your game.

SELECTING THE PROPER CLUB

In Chapter 3 a chart shows the average distances attained with each club by the male amateur player who has learned to execute his golf shots reasonably well.

These distances will be exceeded by many golfers, particularly by a number of the younger and stronger players. For some individuals, however, attaining such distances will be more difficult.

The important thing to learn is *your individual ability* to achieve certain distances with each club in your golf bag. This can be accomplished only by *regular practice* on the driving range, until you feel confident of attaining a consistent distance for each club every time you use it.

One of the glaring faults of many players is the tendency to underclub. That is, they try to hit a ball farther with the club they select than the distance normally to be expected from it. This of course applies mainly to the various irons.

As long as you have decided to equip yourself with a full set of irons you should choose the one for your golf shot that will attain the required distance without pressing or slugging. The manufacturer made your clubs with a particular loft to the clubface for each iron in order to accomplish a certain average distance with that club when properly used. To try to get more distance than normally could be expected from it will generally result in trouble.

NEW GOLF CLUBS*

Standard Lofts

Woods and Irons

Woods	Lofts (Degrees)
1	11
2	13
3	16
4	19
5	22
6	25
7	28

Irons	Lofts (Degrees)
1	17
2	20
3	24
4	28
5	32
6	36
7	40
8	44
9	48
Pitching wedge	52
Sand wedge	56

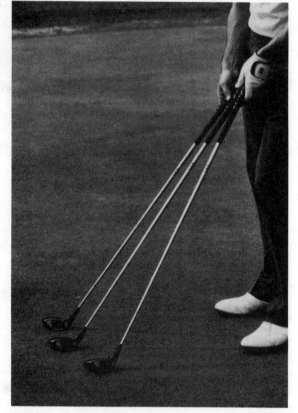

Matched set of modern-day woods.

5	57
6	57 1/2
7	58

Standard Lies

Woods and Irons

Woods	Lie (Degrees)
1	55
2	55 1/2
3	56
4	56 1/2

Irons	Lie (Degrees)
1	55
2	56
3	57
4	58
5	59
6	60
7	61
8	62
9	63
Pitching wedge	63
Sand wedge	63

* The legal limit is "fourteen" clubs in your bag, so let your local professional suggest the right mix suited to your game.

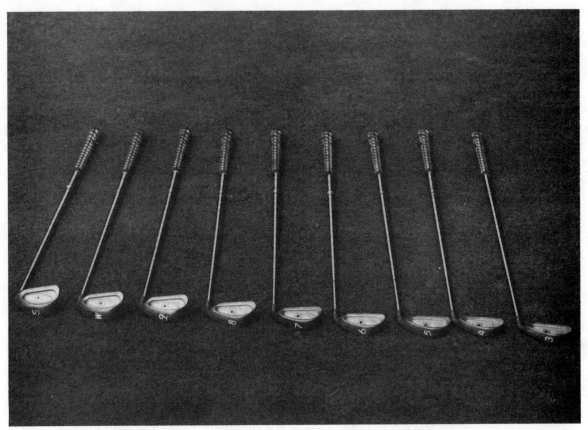

Matched set of modern-day irons. (Unless you're a top-notch golfer, you are better off leaving the 1- and 2-iron out of your bag, and adding a 5-wood, which is easier to hit.)

Standard Lengths

Woods and Irons

Woods	Lengths (Inches)
1	43
2	**42 1/2**
3	**42**
4	**41 1/2**
5	**41**
6	**40 1/2**
7	**40**

Irons	Lengths (Inches)
1	39
2	38 1/2
3	38
4	37 1/2
5	37
6	36 1/2
7	36
8	35 1/2
9	35
Pitching wedge	35
Sand wedge	35

CHOICE OF EQUIPMENT

The Right Ball

1. The average player, particularly the older one, cannot expect to hit the ball as far as professional tournament players or low handicap amateurs.

2. If they wish, they may play with the same highly compressed ball used by professionals, but they may find it is too highly compressed for their particular swing.

3. To attain the best results and distance, choose the ball best suited to *your* particular swing—whether it is *hard, medium,* or *easy.*

4. To qualify this advice, the following explanation may be helpful: At impact, as the clubface strikes the back of the ball, it is compressed (pushed in), or "coiled." As it recoils, it actually *rebounds* off the clubface, giving added impetus, or momentum, to the hit, and to the distance of the ball's flight. (This is another reason why a complete follow-through in the swing is so important.)

    When the player's swing is too easy, the ball cannot be compressed enough for such a recoil. Therefore more distance may be expected when this slow-swinging player uses a lower compressed ball.

5. Keep in mind that when playing in cold weather, a golf ball has less compression than when it is warm. Many professionals warm the ball in their hands before putting it into play.

The Right Club

1. See your teaching professional for the kind of shaft and swing weight that suits *your* personal build and ability.

2. For younger or stronger players, capable of hitting the ball *225 yards or more,* a *stiff* shaft, and swing weight *D-0* to *D-5* is best suited for their wood clubs.

3. If your drive averages *200 yards,* use a *regular* shaft, and swing weight of *C-8* to *D-2.*

4. If your drive carries *175 yards,* use a *flexible* shaft, and swing weight of *C-5* to *C-7.*

5. Older players and women usually get the best results using a *flexible* shaft to gain more clubhead speed.

RENOVATING EQUIPMENT

"Keep the grooves of your woods and irons clean, for a purer strike," is still every top tour pro's motto. It should be yours, too.

More important than getting your golfing paraphernalia to sparkle though, is to preserve it. Giving your shoes, clubheads, grips, shafts, bag, and glove a longer life is what matters most. That is, if you want those favorites to remain favorites.

Maintenance of equipment is not so unlike the disciplines required for grooving a swing; they both call for time and effort. A good procedure to follow is to put your equipment back in order after each day's golf.

Grips are probably one of the most neglected parts of a club. Players forget that perspiration from their hands, dirt, dust at the bottom of the bag, and friction from the clubs rubbing together can affect the life of grips, which are usually made of rubber or leather.

A damp cloth to clean vinyl shoes is still the best remedy for dirt.

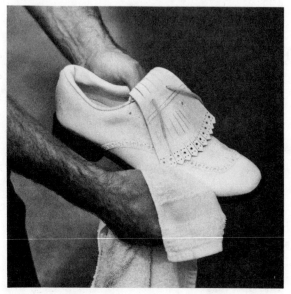

The best way to care for rubber grips is to scrub them with warm soap and water. Repeat this process and dry the grips by rubbing them up and down firmly with a towel.

Although there are various cleaners designed especially for reviving leather grips—saddle soap, for instance—a much more economical way of restoring and retaining the texture is, again, with soap and water. Before applying the soap's lather and letting it sit for a few minutes, use a coarse brush to stimulate the leather. Repeat this once a month to keep the leather in good condition, and to restore leather that has become dry and slippery.

Some golfers use linseed or castor oils to preserve their leather grips. Simply rub the oil in, let the grips sit overnight, so that the oil soaks into the leather, and wipe the oil off the next day.

For keeping leather shoes soft and clean, the best results are still achieved by applying polish and buffing with an old rag or clean cloth.

There are several leather sprays on the market which will serve the purpose when a quick shine is required, but shoe polish still proves the best for treating the leather and for giving a longer-lasting gloss to the shoes. Be sure always to take the time to brush all the grass from around the edges of your shoes; otherwise grit will mix with the polish and scratch the leather.

Vinyl shoes are becoming more and more popular and a wet towel, with or without soap, depending on the severity of the stains, is all that is necessary to keep them clean. Using waterproof polish is a good idea, too.

When replacing a spike or a complete set, be sure to clean the hole in the sole with an old toothbrush, and then apply Vaseline or oil to the spike before tightening it in. With a kit of new spikes a little key will be included in the pack. Nevertheless, it is a good idea to see your pro about a proper spike wrench. You'll find the job much easier, for the

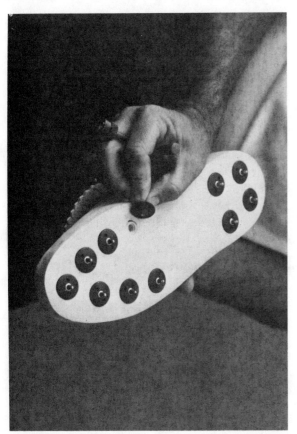

When replacing a spike, pull it out and clean the dirt from the hole.

To replace, screw in the new spike with a special spike wrench, available from your local pro.

wrench has a handle to help your leverage when the spikes are tough to get out.

A good way to maintain your glove is to store it in a sealable plastic bag which will prevent it from getting dry and losing its shape. Another tip is to place a couple of golf balls inside the golf glove to help it to retain its shape; certainly do this when the glove is wet after you've played in the rain.

If you want your leather bag to look smart and be long-lasting, some saddle soap or a special preservative will do the trick.

The best way to maintain a vinyl bag is with soap and water and a soft brush or cloth.

Use a firm brush with soap and water to clean the grooves of your irons. Do not use a wire brush because this will scratch the steel and cause rusting.

To clean your woods, I suggest you use a softer brush and rub not quite so vigorously as you would do when cleaning a cast or forged iron head.

Remember, too, with woods, not to leave the covers on when the heads are wet, or else the wood will swell and the inserts could pop out.

For both persimmon and laminated woods, the best preservative is a good wood polish. Rub on and let set before buffing with a dry cloth.

For aged persimmon heads, soaking them in linseed oil will revitalize them. This is often done by the pros. However, because the swing weight could drastically be affected, it is best for you to check with a clubmaker or pro.

Silver polish will do wonders for your steel shafts.

Learning to care for your equipment has to be a "plus": why else would the pros bother to brush the grass off their shoes, have their caddies wipe the faces of their irons and woods, check their spikes, and keep their grips clean. Besides, if nothing else, clean equipment is a psychological boost.

NEW GOLF CLUBS

A good way to keep your leather glove in "shape" after playing is to place a couple of balls in it.

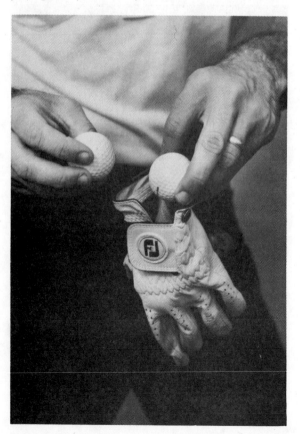

For Women

First, let us assume that the average female amateur player is not as strong physically as the average male. There are exceptions, of course, as evidenced by the fact that many women are capable of hitting golf shots for distances equal to, or frequently farther than, those achieved by many men players.

However, the majority of women must settle for a shorter distance in their golf shots with the various clubs. Accordingly, some women may find that they can attain more distance with higher-lofted wood clubs than with irons.

For those women who can use wood clubs effectively off the fairway, the higher-lofted clubs, such as the Nos. 5, 6, 7, 8, 9, and 10 woods, may help them accomplish the desired results. We strongly urge them, however, to seek the advice of their PGA teaching professional before deciding to use such clubs instead of the proper iron clubs, which are noted for their accuracy when properly used.

In general, women's clubs should have lighter-weight clubheads and the shafts should be more flexible than those used by the average male player, in order to "whip" the clubhead through the ball faster.

The total swing weight, however, should be determined by the golf instructor, in order to fit the club to the ability of the individual woman player.

As a guide, the majority of women will probably find that swing weights of C-6 to C-9 are best suited for their particular swings.

When contemplating the purchase of a new set of clubs, swing with a number of clubs featuring different shaft flexes and swing weights. The right clubs for you are those with which you can hit the longest and most accurate shots.

STARTER SETS

For either the male or female beginner, where economy is often an important factor in the purchase of golf equipment, a starter set of golf clubs is recommended.

While these sets do not contain all of the clubs required for negotiating the various golf shot distances which one will be faced with, they will enable the average beginner to get along fairly well until a full complement of clubs can be acquired.

A starter set usually consists of the following clubs:

> Nos. 1 and 3 woods
> Nos. 3, 5, 7, and 9 irons, and a putter

A typical starter set.

An inexpensive light golf bag should be added to carry the clubs although in some instances such a bag is included in the price. Later on, when a player is ready to buy a complete set of new clubs, a reasonable allowance for the initial starter set can be expected.

Starter sets can be purchased either *new* or *used*. We suggest, however, that you seek the advice of a professional to assure that the clubs you choose, whether new or used, are fitted to *your individual requirements*.

USED "STICKS"

Any pro shop at country clubs, or at municipal and public golf courses, can supply used sets of golf clubs which are *complete for all of the required numbers*. Such clubs may be purchased as is, or fully reconditioned, at various prices, depending on age and quality. The average price for used golf clubs is given at the beginning of this chapter. Of course, these prices vary at different golf courses depending upon the supply and the current market.

Occasionally, many players find that they want to purchase single clubs of various numbers, either woods or irons, which are not included in the set they are presently using. Most pro shops have a rack containing used golf clubs of every possible kind and number, which can generally be bought at a saving.

When purchasing these clubs we suggest that you have a professional help you in the selection, to assure that the *length of the shaft*, the *flexibility*, and the *swing weight* are correct for your particular needs.

If you buy good-quality used clubs in the beginning, and take good care of them, a liberal allowance may be expected when you are ready to purchase a complete *new* set at a later date.

THE RIGHT START FOR YOUNGSTERS

For the youngster who catches the golf "bug," either through watching his or her parents or seeing the top pros playing on television, the amount of equipment required to start off with is really very little—just a few old clubs and a couple of balls.

The clubs can be cut down from a set that Dad no longer uses. It would be unwise to start off with a brand-new set, as the bug may be a passing phase.

Initially, golf is all about developing a feel for hitting the ball, then turning it into a swing, and the basics of this can be learned with the use of only one club. It's worth noting that superstar Seve Ballesteros began playing this way.

Once the ability to handle one club has been mastered, other clubs can be added, and a half set is quite adequate.

Some manufacturers produce junior half sets. Alternatively, a women's half set may be the answer. These will be light enough to handle and the whippy shaft will help with distance. Sets of this nature can easily be obtained secondhand.

The bottom line: don't rush out and buy full-size clubs until you're sure your youngster can handle them, and here again it is well worth keeping an eye out for secondhand bargains in your pro shop and in your local paper.

A NOTE TO PARENTS

Encouragement, common sense, and patience are three essential guidelines for parents to consider if they intend to introduce their son or daughter to the game.

Forcing your child to play golf or to insisting he address the ball or grip the club in a particular way the moment he shows an inkling of enthusiasm will only discourage him.

Possessing the patience to allow your child to follow, first, his natural instincts, is necessary if you want him to develop a growing attraction to golf.

You can bet your best golf ball that when the junior is fed up with merely hitting balls and trying to do things his way he will soon express an interest to learn properly. Kids are no different from adults; they want to find a technique that allows them to repeat the same good swing and hit that same good feeling shot.

The dream of your child growing up to be a superstar on the PGA Tour will have little chance of being realized if a teaching professional doesn't enter the picture somewhere along the line.

Checking to see that your child is following the basics of a sound grip, correct alignment, and keeping his head still will certainly be a positive reinforcement. However, leave the method of instruction and the finer points of the swing to the professional. Too many of today's high handicappers were once juniors who emulated their father's or mother's unorthodox methods.

Lessons do not have to be an expensive proposition either; provided the instructor doesn't have to spend costly time correcting the child's swing faults, acquired while being taught by a friend or a well-intentioned but unqualified parent.

Good teachers will be pleased that a parent is around (not lurking under a nearby tree while the lesson is in progress) as a source of encouragement. You can help by reminding your child to follow the teacher's suggestions for practice drills like hitting shots with the feet together, or following a steady health and fitness program.

Another tip: try and take your child to the practice tee at a professional tournament site. This is where the pros gather prior to a round to groove their swing, or after the round to practice a shot they may have had trouble with during play.

Strategically, the practice tee is the best place for the novice to learn the important aspects of the swing, such as ball position for the different clubs or the keys the pros use to align themselves for the various shots. Here, the junior can see clearly what the pros do; on the course itself, there is often interference from the gallery.

The practice tee is an excellent place then to discover the secrets of rhythm and tempo; the junior will see for himself that a powerful swing isn't a fast hurried one. Juniors who watch the pros soon learn, too, that a good swing depends on good footwork, a strong shoulder turn, and balance.

Because children are great imitators, another strategic place for them to sit in order to learn the ins and outs of a good technique is in front of a television set. Aside from being taught vital swing keys, juniors who watch a telecast of a pro tournament can learn about golf etiquette and the rules.

While learning the game, juniors should always "feel" exactly what each part of the body does, instead of trying to work the swing out by mental steps. The latter can lead to confusion and to a swing lacking continuity.

To summarize, if you have thoughts of teaching your child the game of golf, look around for reputable teachers in your area. See what professional tournaments are being staged near home. Get your TV tuned.

Golf Rules, Etiquette, and "Lingo"

7

G olf is a game to enjoy and, because it is so pleasantly engrossing, one can put everything else out of one's mind and be completely relaxed while playing it.

Just how seriously must you take the game? The answer is, just as seriously as you wish to take it, except that you should never allow this or any other sport to make you tense, intolerant, unpleasant, or uncompanionable.

Many of those with whom you play have been playing the game for a number of years and are familiar with the rules of golf, golf etiquette, and the language of the sport. You should be, too, to enjoy golf even more and to spare yourself possible embarrassment.

We suggest that you purchase a copy of the latest United States Golf Association Rules. They may be obtained at your golf course pro shop at a very nominal cost. The more you follow the rules of golf play, and of golf etiquette—and know the "lingo" —the more certain it is that you will become a desirable playing companion.

Two of the most flagrant violations of good etiquette are the *failure to replace divots* in the fairway and ball marks on the green. Good players *always* do, and you can win the respect of your playing companions and help to keep your favorite golf course in better shape if you not only replace your own divots and ball marks, but also those overlooked by less thoughtful players.

To help you become a better-educated player more quickly, we've designed the following "crash course" on golf rules, etiquette, and terminology.

KNOW THE CORRECT U.S.G.A. RULE IN SIX COMMON COURSE SITUATIONS

Bending or Breaking Branches

SITUATION: The ball lies near trees and overhanging branches.

INCORRECT: To make his swing less awkward, the player bends or breaks some branches.

CORRECT: Rule 13-2: "Except as provided in the Rules, a player shall not improve or allow to be improved the area of his intended swing or his line of play by moving, bending, or breaking anything growing or fixed, including objects defining out of bounds."

NOTE: "If these circumstances occur when a player fairly takes his stance, makes a stroke or the backward movement of his club for a stroke, there is no penalty."

Unplayable Lie

SITUATION: The player's ball lies at the base of a tree; he's stymied.

Player breaking *The Rules of Golf* by breaking branches.

A typical unplayable lie.

When facing an unplayable lie, you should never toss the ball out sideways. Abide by Rule 28.

INCORRECT: The player tosses the ball several yards from the spot, takes a penalty of 1 stroke, and plays the next shot.

CORRECT: Rule 28: "If a player deems his ball to be unplayable, he shall, under penalty of one stroke: a. Play his next stroke as nearly as possible at the spot from which the original ball was last played (Rule 20-5); or b. Drop a ball within two club lengths of the spot where the ball lay, but not nearer the hole; or c. Drop a ball behind the point where the ball lay, keeping that point directly between the hole and the spot on which the ball is dropped, with no limit to how far behind the point the ball may be dropped."

Lost Ball Time Limit

SITUATION: The player looks for his ball in deep rough.

INCORRECT: He finds the ball after 5 minutes have gone by and plays on, ignorant of the rule.

CORRECT: Rule 27 (Definition: a) "A ball is lost if: a. It is not found or identified as his by the player within five minutes after the player's side or his or their caddies have begun to search for it."

NOTE: Penalty—stroke and distance exactly as I have here.

Ground Club in Hazard

SITUATION: Player's approach lands in a bunker.

INCORRECT: While addressing the ball, the player's clubhead touches the sand. He plays on, unaware that he has broken a rule.

CORRECT: Rule 13-4: "Before making a stroke at a ball which lies in or touches a hazard (whether a bunker or a water hazard), the player shall not: b. Touch the ground in a hazard or water in the water hazard with a club or otherwise."

Waiving the Rules

SITUATION: In a match, a player discovers at the second hole that he has one extra club in his bag— 15 instead of the maximum of 14 allowed under Rule 4-4a.

INCORRECT: His opponent refuses to apply the penalty. The extra club is declared out of play and the match continues.

CORRECT: Rule 1-3: "Players shall not agree to exclude the operation of any Rule or to waive any penalty incurred."

FOOTNOTE: The penalty for breach of Rule 1-3 in matchplay is disqualification of both sides.

Out of Bounds

SITUATION: The player hits an errant shot that finishes out-of-bounds.

INCORRECT: The player drops the ball back in play, next to the spot where it went out of bounds and penalizes himself 1 stroke.

CORRECT: Rule 27-1: "If a ball is out of bounds, the player shall play a ball, under penalty of one stroke, as nearly as possible at the spot from which the original ball was last played (See Rule 20-5)."

THE 12 GOLDEN RULES OF GOLF ETIQUETTE

1. No one should move or talk, or stand close to, or directly behind, the ball or hole when a player is making a stroke.

2. The player who has the honor should be allowed to play before his opponent tees his ball.

3. Golfers should play without undue delay. However, no player should hit until the party in front is out of range.

4. When play has been completed, players should immediately leave the putting green.

5. Players looking for a lost ball should allow other players coming up to pass them. They should signal such players to pass, and should not continue to play until the passing players are out of range.

6. A player should replace and press down all divots cut by him. Also, he should repair ball marks on the green.

7. Players should carefully fill or smooth all holes or footmarks made by them in sand traps.

8. Players should see that neither they nor their caddies injure the surface of the green by standing close to the hole when the ground is soft, or when replacing the flagstick.

9. A player who has incurred a penalty should indicate this to his opponent as soon as possible.

10. Players whose balls have reached the green should not leave their carts or golf bags on any part of that green.

11. A player should not walk in front or ahead of others in his group who have not completed their shots. This is not only dangerous, but is disturbing to those about to make their strokes.

12. *Be a good sport!* Compliment your opponent when he makes a good shot.

GLOSSARY OF GOLFING TERMS

ACE: Hitting the first shot from the tee into the hole.

ADDRESS: The position taken by a player when preparing to start a stroke.

AIR SHOT: Missing the ball. Also: "whiff."

ALBATROSS: A score, on a hole, of 3 shots under par. Also: "double eagle."

AMATEUR: A person who plays golf as a sport, not as a profession.

APPROACH: Second shot to a par 4, or third shot to a par 5, usually played with an iron club.

APRON: The low-cut grassy area immediately surrounding a green.

ARMY GOLF: A tongue-in-cheek expression. A golfer plays "army golf" if he hits one shot that flies left, another right, another left, and so on. Thus, the marching lingo: left-right, left-right, left-right.

AWAY: The golfer who is farthest from the hole, or "away," plays first.

BACK DOOR: A putted ball that falls in the "back door" is one that rolls around the hole, and when it looks like it will stay out, drops in the back of the hole.

BACK SIDE: The second or "inward" 9 holes of a regulation golf course.

BACKSPIN: The reverse spin imparted on the ball to make it "bite," or stop quickly.

BALL POSITION: The spot where the ball is placed in the stance. Example: opposite the left heel.

BANANA BALL: A wild shot that curves to the right in the shape of a banana.

BENT: A finely textured grass.

BERMUDA: A coarsely textured grass.

BIRDIE: The score for a hole played in 1 stroke under par.

BLAST: Recovering from a sand bunker by impacting the sand with the clubhead, and lifting the ball by moving or "blasting" the shot. Blasting is used synonymously with "exploding."

BLIND HOLE: If a player hits an ideal drive and the green is not visible, the hole is said to be "blind."

BOGEY: A score of 1 stroke above par for the hole.

BOLD: A shot played too firmly. Usually a putt rolled several feet past the hole.

BRASSIE: A No. 2 wood.

BREAK: The curve in a green. When a player putts,

he allows for the "break."

BURIED LIE: A ball embedded in the sand. Called a "fried egg" if the lie is severe.

CADDIE: A person who carries a player's clubs and assists him in club selection and strategy.

CAN: To knock a putt in the hole.

CARRY: The distance measured from the place where the ball is hit to the point it first touches the ground.

CASUAL WATER: Any temporary accumulation of water (such as a puddle) not regarded as a water hazard. The Rules of Golf permit a player to lift his ball from casual water without penalty.

CHIP: A low shot played from the fringe of the green with an iron.

CHOKE: To grip down on the club. Also: to crack under pressure.

CLUBBING A PLAYER: To advise a golfer which club to play for a particular shot.

CLUBFACE: The hitting portion of a club, featuring grooves.

CLUBHOUSE: A building with locker, bar, and restaurant facilities, situated near the first tee and eighteenth green.

COCKED WRISTS: The bending of the wrists during the swing.

COURSE: The land on which golf is played.

CUT ONE IN: To work a high shot, from left to right, so it lands softly on the green.

DEAD: A ball that finishes next to the hole.

DEAD-STYMIED: A player's shot lands in a trouble spot, leaving him no swing.

DIVOT: A slice of turf cut from the fairway by a player's club.

DOGLEG: A hole that curves to the left or right, rather dramatically.

DORMIE: A situation in a match when a player or team is as many holes ahead as remain to be played. Opponent(s) must win every remaining hole(s) to tie the match.

DOUBLE BOGEY: A score of 2 over par for a hole.

DOWN: The number of holes (match play) a player is behind an opponent. Also: a ball buried or sitting "down" in the grass.

DOWNSWING: Swinging the club from the top of the swing to impact.

DRAW: A shot that flies with a slight curve from right to left.

DRIVE: To hit a ball from a tee, usually with a No. 1 wood.

DUCK HOOK: A low shot that starts its flight left of the target line, and flies farther left, hitting the ground quickly.

DUFFER: An unskilled player or "hacker."

EAGLE: A score of 2 strokes under par for a hole.

EMBEDDED BALL: A ball buried in soft or wet turf.

FADE: A ball that flies on a slight curve, from left to right.

FAIRWAY: The mowed area of the course between the tee and the putting green.

FAT: A weak shot that occurs when the club digs deep into the turf behind the ball. Also: "scuff." A fat chip is called a "chili-dip."

FINISH: The final part of the swing, when the club moves upward again.

FLAGSTICK: A movable pole placed in the hole to show its location on the green.

FLANGE: The additional surface of the clubhead which protrudes at the bottom or "sole."

FLIER: A ball that flies without spin, going farther than normal, because of wet grass or moisture on the clubface.

FOLLOW-THROUGH: Driving the clubhead through the ball after the moment of impact.

FORE: Warning cry to persons in danger of getting hit by a ball.

FORECADDIE: A person employed by a tournament committee to spot and mark a ball, especially on blind holes and in areas of heavy rough.

FOUR-BALL: A match in which two golfers play their better ball against the better ball of two opponents.

FOURSOME: A match in which two play against two, and each team plays 1 ball. Format: alternate tee shots, alternate shots. Also: four golfers playing together.

FRONT SIDE: The first or "outward" 9 holes on a regulation course.

GIMME: In match play, a putt so short that it is usually conceded by an opponent. Not allowed during stroke play competition.

GRAIN: The direction that grass grows in on a putting green.

GREEN: The flat low-cut surface that players putt on.

GREEN FEE: The money paid for the privilege of playing a course.

GREENSIDE: The area surrounding a green.

GRIP: The part of the shaft covered with rubber or leather, by which the club is grasped.

GROSS: The total number of strokes on a hole or course before a player's handicap is deducted.

HALVED: In match play, a hole or game is "halved" when two players, or teams, tie.

HAZARD: A bunker or body of water on a golf course.

HEAD: The part of the club with which the ball is struck, consisting of the neck, heel, toe, sole, and face.

HOLE: A round receptacle in the green, 4 1/4 inches in diameter, at least 4 inches deep, and usually metal-lined.

HOLE-HIGH: A ball finishing even with the hole, off to one side.

HOLE-OUT: Knocking the ball into the hole, from anywhere on the course.

HOME: The green.

HONOR: The privilege of hitting first from a tee. Accorded to the winner of the previous hole.

HOOD: When you hood the clubface, you deloft it by pointing it more toward the ground than the sky.

HOOK: A shot that veers sharply from right to left.

HOSEL: The hollow part of an iron clubhead, into which a shaft is fitted.

IN-THE-LEATHER: In a friendly match, a player will usually concede a putt that lies no farther from the hole than the length of the leather wrapping on a putter.

LAG: To hit a long putt with the intention of leaving the ball close to the hole.

LATERAL HAZARD: A water hazard that runs approximately parallel to the line of play.

LIE: The position in which a ball rests on the ground. Also: the angle the shaft makes with the ground, when the club is soled, or sitting in the natural position.

LIP: The rim of the hole, or bunker.

LOFT: The degree of pitch built into the clubface and designed to lift the ball into the air.

MAKING THE TURN: When a player completes the front nine and moves on to the tenth tee.

MATCH PLAY: A competition by holes. Example: player A beats player B on the first hole and goes one-up. They tie the remaining holes. Thus, player A wins one-up.

MEDAL: A competition of stroke play format. Player adds total scores for 18 holes.

MULLIGAN: A try-again shot, usually off the first tee. Common only in friendly matches, but illegal according to The Rules of Golf.

NECK: The part of a wooden club—where the shaft

joins the clubhead.

NET: A player's score, once his handicap is deducted.

ON THE SWEET SPOT: Hitting the ball dead center on the clubface. Also: "on the screws."

OUT-OF-BOUNDS: The ground on which play is prohibited.

OVERCLUBBING: Hitting with too much club. Example: playing a No. 8 iron when the shot calls for a No. 9.

PAR: The number of strokes an excellent player should take for a hole.

PARALLEL POSITION: The clubshaft, at the top of the swing, is parallel to the target line.

PASS: In the downswing, the movement of the lower body through impact.

PENALTY STROKE: A stroke added to a player's score for violating the rules.

PITCH: An approach shot hit with a lofted club, usually a pitching wedge. The ball flies high and stops quickly.

PITCH-AND-RUN: A short pitch shot that flies low, lands, and rolls up to the flag.

PLAYING THROUGH: A group of players given permission to pass a slower group playing ahead.

POT BUNKER: A deep sand trap.

PROVISIONAL: A ball played after a previous shot is believed to be lost or out of bounds.

PULL: A ball that flies left of the target, with little or no curving action.

PUNCH: A low controlled shot, played with a shorter swing.

PUSH: A ball that flies to the right of the target with little or no curving.

PUTT: A stroke made on the green with a putter.

REGULATION FIGURES: Hitting a par-3 hole in one shot. Hitting a par-4 hole in two shots. Hitting a par-5 in three shots. Add the regulation two putts per hole to each, and the score is par.

RUB OF THE GREEN: This occurs when a ball in motion is stopped or deflected by an outside agency. Whether the result goes for or against the player depends on the element of luck.

SANDBAGGER: An adept golfer who plays well below his handicap when money is on the line.

SCRATCH: A player who receives no handicap allowance.

SHAFT: The part of the club which is not the clubhead.

SKULL: To hit a poor, fast running shot, usually with a short iron, by contacting the ball with the leading edge of the clubhead.

SKY: A very high shot.

SNAKE: An extremely long putt that winds back and forth over the several undulations in the green.

SOCKET: Golf's ugliest shot. This occurs when the hosel of the club or socket contacts the ball, causing it to shoot dead right. Also called a "shank."

SOLE: The bottom of the clubhead. Also: grounding the club at address.

SOLE PLATE: The metal plate located at the bottom of a driving club.

STANCE: The position of a player's feet when he addresses the ball.

STROKE HOLE: A hole(s) at which a player applies a handicap stroke. The scorecard designates stroke holes.

SUDDEN DEATH: Tied matches are broken by a sudden-death playoff—the continuation of a match or stroke play competition ending as soon as one player wins a hole.

SUMMER RULES: Golfers play the ball as it lies.

SWING: The action by a player in stroking the ball.

TAKEAWAY: The start of the backswing. When the player moves the clubhead low to the ground.

TEE: A peg on which a ball is placed. Also: the teeing ground.

TEXAS WEDGE: A shot played from off the green, usually from a low-lipped bunker or the apron, with a putter.

THREAD THE NEEDLE: Hitting a shot through a narrow opening.

TOE: The part of the clubhead farthest from where it joins the shaft. Also: to hit the ball to the right, by contacting it with the "toe" of the club.

TOP: To strike the ball above center.

TRAP: A pit or depression filled with sand.

UNDERCLUBBING: Using a club that will not reach the green. Example: hitting with a No. 9, when the shot calls for an 8.

UNPLAYABLE LIE: A ball in such an awkward position that the player chooses to take relief.

UP: In match play, the number of holes a player is ahead of an opponent. Also: a ball sitting "up" in the grass.

WAGGLE: The preliminary movement of the club or the body prior to the actual swing.

WIND CHEATER: A low hit ball that pierces a headwind.

WINTER RULES: A ball lying on any "closely mown area" through the green may, without penalty, be moved or may be lifted, cleaned, and placed within 6 inches of where it originally lay, but not nearer the hole.

YIP STROKE: A nervous jab of the putterblade on the ball.

About the Authors

John Andrisani

John Andrisani is senior editor of golf instruction at *Golf Magazine*. Formerly, he was assistant editor of the London-based *Golf Illustrated*. With 1985 British Open Champion Sandy Lyle, Andrisani is the author of *Learning Golf: The Lyle Way* and, with superstar Seve Ballesteros, *Natural Golf*. A recent holder of the American Golf Writer's Championship, Andrisani plays off an eight handicap at Siwanoy Country Club, in Westchester County, New York.

Frank Kenyon Allen

Frank Kenyon Allen joined the Cameron Park Country Club in 1967 and eventually became its president. He was an avid golfer who enjoyed a handicap of ten even in his seventies.

Tom Lo Presti

Recognized as one of the finest teachers of the game, "Tommy" Lo Presti has devoted his life to the task of helping others learn the fine points of the golf swing. Lo Presti has been head professional at Haggin Oaks Golf Course in Sacramento, California, for fifty-five years. Always willing to help golfers of all ages—and handicaps—he still can't be pulled off the lesson tee, even today.

Dale Mead

Dale Mead served as head professional at Del Rio Country Club in Modesto, California, for nineteen years. In 1981 he was named Northern California Golf Professional of the Year.

Barbara Romack

As a former U.S. Women's Amateur champion and winner on the Ladies' Professional Golf Association Tour, Barbara Romack is eminently qualified to offer her advice on all aspects of the game. Romack currently teaches golf at Atlantis Country Club, near Palm Beach, Florida.